BARBARA

THE
BASIC
GUIDE
TO THE
FEELER
GIFT

I dedicate this book to my children.
They are my cheerleaders,
whose support and applause
are lovingly appreciated.

And also to the many feelers
who have been misunderstood.
I 'feel' you.

CONTENTS

ACKNOWLEDGMENTS

To Chelsea Slade, my editor. A huge thank you and acknowledgment for her expertise and immense patience. I cannot tell you how many times this manuscript went back and forth with the editing and complexity of developing the chapters. She is extraordinary.

Andrea Petry: Once again I thank you friend. She gave her time and expertise to this manuscript, getting this project into book form. She talked in knowledgeable terms as though it was a foreign language to me. I am forever thankful for this divine friendship.

To the many who have contributed to this project and were included in this book. I was captivated by their experiences and their stories and fell deeper into love with the Lord through their eyes. It unveiled God in a whole different realm, and I was able to see the magnitude of God through their eyes. Everyone has a perspective of who God is and what He is all about, but it is refreshing to hear others describe who He is to themselves. God unveils Himself in different and amazing ways in our journey with Him. I am deeply thankful to my friends and community that allows me to peek inside of their world and see another side of God. How great is He!

Thank you to Alyssa Hughey at Printopya. This is truly an amazing company to interact with and I highly recommend them for book printing, typesetting, and project management services. Alyssa was incredibly patient with my many questions and completely professional. She is a joy to work with.

Acknowledgements to my proofreaders, Emory Hornaday and Michele Hogan. Immense insight and feedback. I appreciate you, more than you will ever know.

Thank you Pastor Gerardo Ramos who gave me the freedom and trust to expand in my gifts through the Holy Spirit.

INTRODUCTION

This book is written to a special and unique population in God's Kingdom: The Feelers. Many people have heard the phrase "feeler," but they have no concept of what that is, or what to do with it. Is it a gift? If so, how can God give a gift of feelings? Most people are familiar with the gifts of a seer, or a prophetic gifting, but the feeler gift is virtually unknown.

There have been multiple books written on the gifts of the Holy Spirit: teacher, prophet, healer, etc. Paul writes about the spiritual gifts in 1 Corinthians 12, and they are mentioned throughout the New Testament. But there are gifts that God has given that are not listed in the Bible, or they are more obscure.

My goal is to tackle and put words to the gift of the feeler. Feelings are very difficult to describe. For example, you can describe the symptoms of love, and poets and authors have spent a lifetime trying. We can describe the heart-thumping, stomach-fluttering feeling of love, but the actual emotion of love is difficult to put into words. This is what I am attempting to do with the Feeler Gift of the Holy Spirit. You may know that you have a gift, that God is speaking to you through your emotions, but how do you describe that to others in a tangible way? It is like trying to grab water as it is flowing past you in a creek. It flows through your fingers, you can't quite grasp it, but you feel it's cool wetness.

I first began exploring this idea of the feeler gift after years of experiencing unexplainable shifts in emotion depending on my environment. I would perceive things about people and situations without understanding that God was speaking to me through my feelings. Throughout various careers and ups and downs in my relationship with God, I slowly began to recognize that my feelings and perceptions were a gift.

It wasn't until I attended my first year of Bethel School of Supernatural Ministry (BSSM) in Redding, California in 2015, that I had context for this gift that I had been walking in for years. It was like massive puzzle pieces that seem to click into place. I had understanding and had verbiage for what I had been experiencing most of my life.

When I was in my third year at BSSM, I began to mentor other students. Through this process, I realized that many of them had no idea about the feeler gift. I decided to offer classes that I called "Field Trips." I would invite students to meet me at a coffee shop where we would sit and talk about the gift: what it is, why it exists, and what to do with it. Then I would take them to the Redding library or the local Walmart. The library had many "characters" that spent time there, along with the many homeless people who were there and in the neighboring park. Walmart was simply large enough to wander through and explore our feelings. In fact, in Walmart, we quickly noticed that each department carried its own environment and emotional climate. Because of this, the library and the store were two places that a feeler could easily feel something. Afterward, we would debrief and share what it was we experienced on our field trip. In this way, the students began to learn how to use their gift. I continued this method of teaching up until the time the Lord prompted me to write this book.

For the people who have lived with intense feelings and emotions, not knowing what to do with them, this book is for you. For those of you who do not know how to "deal with" the emotional people in your life, this is a good book to help you understand them and be a comfort and support to them. This will help you walk a mile in their shoes and be a little more knowledgeable about what they are dealing with. For the ones who know you have the feeler gift, this book will expand the language you use to explain the unexplainable emotions and feelings happening in your world and help you navigate this gift.

If you are curious and wondering if this gift applies to you; yes, it does. I believe everyone is a feeler in one way or another. A feeler has emotions, and I am sure you do too. You can love, or be perturbed, or experience sorrow. These are all emotions of a feeler.

The *feeler gift*, however, takes our experience of these emotions into a whole different realm of possibility—opening us up to explore the things God wants us to feel and the gift He wants us to walk in. As you journey through this book and uncover the feeler gift, you will be peeking into the spiritual realm. How fabulous is that!

I have talked with many believers, both new and mature, about understanding their feeler gifting. The more I learned about my own gifting, the more I desired to help other feelers walk in authority and clarity. As you join me on this journey, I pray I will be able to answer most of your questions. Together, we will explore what the gift of the feeler is, where it comes from, and how to use and grow your gift as you deepen your relationship with God.

You will receive input and testimonies from my own experiences as well as from several other sources, and do you know why? Because as God gives gifts to individuals, He is gracious enough to install and anoint gifts upon us in a manner that is unique to us. There is no one-size-fits-all gift from God. How we understand and operate in our gifting will look slightly different from person to person. We are all individuals that have different gifts and different anointings. That is what makes us so special. And He does this because we are unique, and He makes every gifting a special gift.

God gives gifts for a purpose. That is what this book was written for: to put words to the definition and purpose of the feeler gift. You are immensely anointed to have this gift, even though, at this point, you may not feel like it is a gift you carry. Once you realize that you wield a powerful weapon that can be used for the Kingdom and against the enemy, you will understand its uniqueness and purpose.

As we begin this adventure into unwrapping the gift of the feeler, I want to make sure you understand that God has crafted this special gift with you in mind. He has individualized this gift for you to use as part of His plan for you.

Most of all, I want to take this opportunity to praise God for being a fantastic gift giver.

Bless you.

CHAPTER ONE

FEELER

The first time I ever visited the Oregon Country Fair was in 2013. The hippy, new-age, Renaissance, spiritualist festival was different than I expected. I thought it would be like a country fair: popcorn, caramel apples, and hot dogs. But instead, it was something else entirely. The fair felt like torment to my spirit.

I immediately felt a heaviness when I entered the fairgrounds, even though everyone around me was gaily partying and romping. Yes, I said romping! This fair was interesting, to say the least. Partial nudity, drugs, people walking around in outfits that depicted fairies or mystical beings, their bodies painted in an array of colors. It was 400 acres of genuinely nice craft booths, over 200 food venues, and several music venues. Even though I like to people watch, the Oregon Country Fair overloaded my senses.

My first visit was with my youngest daughter, Madeline, who was overjoyed at all the shopping possibilities. While she reveled in the different craft booths, I struggled with the atmosphere—especially one alley. That particular row of booths also included an altar, inviting customers to pray to a specific deity. I tried my hardest to shield myself and my emotions, but I felt exhausted. The crafts were wonderful, and the music was good, but I was constantly in a battle with my feelings.

Near the end of the day, we stopped at a music venue to listen before we exited the fair. There were hay bales placed around the dance floor, which I stood on so that I could look over the area. I watched the white clad dancers on the stage and felt like something was not right. I began to watch one woman dancing seductively. I noticed that as she danced with a man, he would begin to manifest demonically. She would move on and dance with another man, and the process repeated. I began to pray over the area, the dancers, that particular woman, and the men she engaged with. I was praying, declaring, doing warfare, and breaking off assignments.

Suddenly, my daughter grabbed my arm and started nervously pulling me away. She wanted to get out of there. As we were walking out of the fair, she asked me, "Did you see what just happened?"

"No, what do you mean?" I said.

"Mom, didn't you see the guy that was right in front of you?" I shook my head no. "He was dressed as a warlock, and he was cursing you. He was standing right in front of you, Mom."

I hadn't seen him at all. It was as though God shielded him from me.

WHAT IS A FEELER?

A feeler is someone who feels intense emotions that may or may not be their own. They can feel completely content in one moment, and then walk into a different room and feel suddenly frustrated, overwhelmed, or discouraged the next.

You may say, "That sounds like everyone!" Yep, it could be, but many feelers are described as "sensitive" or "over-emotional." And most of the time they are described this way simply because they become overstimulated by their environment and surrounding atmosphere, and they don't yet have the tools to manage the gift.

The feeler gift can make you feel vulnerable, and you are constantly trying to manage it, not realizing that it may be the environment or other factors that are causing you to feel that way.

If you can relate to my rollercoaster of emotions at the fair or my simple definition above, then chances are God is speaking to you through your emotions, you just haven't realized it yet. Or maybe you have, and you are eager to better understand His heart for you and your gifting.

The feeler gift is multi-dimensional and as you delve into this book, you will find information for the beginning feelers and also for the ones that know they walk in this gifting. As stated in the introduction, this gift has many layers and everyone is unique. God gives gifts for His purpose.

I wasn't always so aware of my emotions and their connection to the atmospheres and people around me. Yet, discerning and "feeling" have always been part of my makeup. Years ago, my husband was an entrepreneur and was constantly meeting with potential investors for business and real estate opportunities. Having recognized my gift of "intuition"—as we understood it at the time—he would use me to discern situations in business and "feel out" different people and opportunities during the business meetings.

There were many times that I would go to a meeting just so he could ask afterwards what I perceived. For part of our marriage, we were not Christians, and even when we accepted the Lord as our Savior, I still did not know about the Holy Spirit and how He operated. I was operating in the gifts of the Holy Spirit without knowing what these gifts were.

It wasn't until my first year at Bethel School of Supernatural Ministry (BSSM) in Redding, California that I began to learn what a "feeler" is. I was simply trying to learn more about God. I was already operating in the gift of deliverance before attending Bethel, but God began to "un-box" Himself when I was in BSSM. I had heard people talk about "feeling" what was around them, spiritually and this idea of my experiences being a gift began to evolve.

Because this is a new concept for many people, I will start at the beginning and explain some foundations of both the gift and the Kingdom of God. From this foundational knowledge of Christ and His Kingdom, we will expand our understanding of the feeler gift, how to use it, and why God chose us to carry such a gift.

THE GIFTS ARE FROM GOD

First and foremost, we need to acknowledge that this gift is from the One and Only God Almighty. We'll dive deeper into the biblical evidence of the feeler gift in later chapters, but before even that, we must understand where this gift comes from.

You can choose to say the feeler gift (or any gift) is from Father God, or Jesus Christ, or from the Holy Spirit. I am not going to nitpick about which one of the Trinity this gift comes from because it comes from the One True God. I pray that we can all agree on that. Therefore, whichever One of the Trinity I choose to talk about concerning this gift, please believe that I am talking inclusively, saying all of the Trinity is involved.

At times I will mention God, Holy Spirt, and Christ—often we acknowledge a certain member of the Trinity based on our experience or the ways in which God is working in our hearts at the time. James 1:17 (NIV) says, "Every good and perfect gift is from above, coming down from the Father of the heavenly lights, who does not change like shifting shadows." Our God, who is three in one, is the giver of all good gifts, including this one. It is from this place that we can build our understanding of the feeler gift.

WE ARE ALL FEELERS

Another foundational belief is that everyone is a feeler, to one degree or another, and we all feel emotions. We all have the capacity to hear from God and be used by Him through our feelings. Just as we all have the capacity to prophesy, though we may not all be prophets.

The feeler *gift*, however, is directed to unique individuals that can discern emotions and patterns in both the spiritual and physical realm. It does not matter whether you are male or female. If you are a human being, you can have the feeler gift. There are levels in this gift, just like there are levels in the gift of prophecy. High-level feelers can be born with this gift but also develop it throughout their lifetime. Others become aware of this gift later in life and God will use them profoundly to walk as feelers as they also develop this gift.

Paul talks about the gift of prophecy as something to be sought (1 Corinthians 14:1). This indicates that prophecy can be developed. There are feelers who are born with this gift, but just like prophecy, it can also be developed. Paul writes, "Since you are eager for the gifts of the Spirit, try to excel in those that build up the church" (1 Corinthians 14:12). We are all feelers, and we can all ask for and seek to excel in this gift that has been given to build up the church!

THE BIBLE IS THE WORD OF GOD

Another foundational point we must agree upon is that the Bible is the Word of God. I may bring in other quotes from writers, pastors, and speakers, but the bedrock of our belief is the Bible, the written Word of God. I understand there are many translations of the Bible, but the essence of what the Lord is telling us flows throughout the Old and New Testaments and His consistency is apparent, even if the words may be a little different.

In his book, *Rooted*, Banning Liebscher talks about our own walk with the Lord. "In order to develop a thriving root system, our lives must be rooted in the soil of Scripture…the mandate for every Christian is first and foremost to follow Jesus. But we won't know where to follow Jesus unless we see where He is going, and the first place to discover where Jesus is going is found in the Bible."

We must yearn in wanting intimacy with God. This is our life-time goal, to develop a relationship with the Lord. Our relation-ship begins with time spent with Jesus, reading what He has to say through Scripture, and talking to Him. Personally, I am always asking Jesus questions. I am like a two-year-old, always asking why, who, and what. This goes on throughout the day. Sometimes I get an answer and sometimes I don't. But if the question is important enough to me, I then search out the answer. Jesus loves that. It's called hunger and passion. He is talking ALL the time, but are we tuning in our senses to what He is saying?

There are several books about how to develop intimacy with God, therefore I will not rehash what has already been said. But what I do want to emphasize is that it is vitally important to have a relationship and hear what God has to say. Know His voice! Once you know His voice, you can determine when you are hearing (or feeling) anything that is not from Him.

As with any gift, there are times when the gift will rule over us. This is especially true as we deal with the emotions of the feeler gift. In order to navigate those moments, we must have Jesus Christ—not our gift—as our head. I highly encourage you to spend time with the Lord every day. We must "root" our walk with God in the Scriptures and in our daily devotions—the secret place with the Lord.

JESUS WILL RETURN

Within the written Word of God, we learn that Jesus Christ is the Messiah, the Savior, Anointed One, and God Himself. Everything in creation hinges on who He says He is. Even the rocks would scream out who He is (Luke 19:40).

This leads us to my last fundamental foundation of the Christian belief: that Jesus promised to come again. Revelation 22:7 says, "Look, I am coming soon! Blessed is the one who keeps the words of the prophecy written in this scroll." And Rev 22:12-13 and 16 says, "Look, I am coming soon! My reward is with me, and I will give to each person according to what they have done. I am the Alpha and Omega, the First and the Last, the Beginning and the End ...I, Jesus, have sent my angel to give you this testimony for the churches. I am the Root and the Offspring of David, and the bright Morning Star."

I love how Jesus shouts out His name and authority throughout the book of Revelation, the last book in the Bible. The Old and New Testaments are full of His titles and who He is. Our worship of His name is fundamental and anticipating His return is where we need to press forward with developing and interacting with our gifts. We are not to be inactive in our waiting but be active in our anticipation of completing things that only we can do on earth.

There are times when I am waiting to board a plane, or for the plane to take off, and I play mindless games on my iPhone. It is my attempt to try to temporarily redirect my active mind. I "feel" my environment and have shielded myself, but I need a moment of reprieve, especially if I am in a crowded area. One particular game wants you to dump objects into a pit in order to eliminate everything on your board. During this game, there is a timer that is ticking away, and as the clock clicks downward to zero seconds,

I begin to rush my little objects into a pit. I have observed that as the timer gets down to finish the game, I rush even more. Recently, the Lord interrupted the game and said, this is what is happening in the last days. I realized that we need to accelerate the rate of our anticipation.

We are anticipating the Lord coming. This is whether He comes in our lifetime, during the last trumpet calling, or whether we take our last breath on earth. I anticipate His coming with excitement and urgency to complete tasks that He is giving me. And the tasks may be as simple as intimacy with Him, or to rest in His arms. Even these tasks are important! It is wonderful to discover everything about Him. It is like hunting for gold, which, in fact, you and I are doing just that: discovering more and more about Him as we eagerly anticipate His return.

THE FOUNDATIONS OF THE FEELER GIFT

For most of us, these simple foundational beliefs are taken for granted. You would be amazed, however, at how many people feel differently about each one of these foundations. Yet, the undisputed truth of the Bible remains. There is one God, and the Godhead consists of three parts, the Father, Jesus the Son, and the Holy Spirit.

Jesus Christ is the begotten Son of God, who came from heaven. Mary, Jesus' mother, was a virgin when conceived by the Holy Spirit and continued to be a virgin until she gave birth to Jesus. He is the pure and sinless Lamb to be sacrificed for mankind on the cross, and He received back the keys that Adam gave away to Satan. Jesus rose from the dead after three days and is now alive and sits at the right hand of the Father. The price was paid in full for our sins by the work of Jesus on the cross, and we cannot work our way into salvation but only through grace, repentance, forgiveness, and the belief in Jesus Christ.

If you can say "Yes" and "Amen!" to these foundations, then I believe your heart is prepared to fully grab hold of what it is to be a feeler, walk in the gift of the feeler, or support those around you who have this gift.

BEGIN WITH A FRESH PERSPECTIVE

There is one more thing I believe we need to do to begin this journey with an open mind. We must begin with a fresh perspective of this gift. I want you to be proactive in hearing from God and learning from Him. This is God's heart desire, to have an intimate relationship with you. His love burns for you and your friendship.

With this fresh perspective, there are two prayers that I would like you to consider praying. That is, only if they pertain to you and you choose to do so. God is all about the freedom of choices and this is one of those choices that you get to walk through.

One prayer is the prayer of repentance. For those of us who feel that we have been given a gift from God but have shut down our gifting, I believe we need to ask the Lord to forgive us. I have a prescribed prayer that will help you, if needed.

The other prayer is the prayer to ask Him for the gift to be returned or be awakened. Some people have asked for their feelings to go away or be shut down, not realizing that they are part of the gift that the Lord has given them. Sometimes we have mismanaged the gift due to lack of knowledge, or the enemy has twisted its proper use. We just could not handle it and have said the words, "go away." It is time to take back the gift that the Lord has lovingly kept on hold for you. Now is the time to learn its uses.

(Note: Be sure to say all prayers in this book out loud. You can whisper, if needed, but it must be done orally. I will explain about this later in the book.)

PRAYER OF REPENTANCE:

Holy Lord, I repent for rejecting or shutting down the gift you have given me. I did not know what I didn't know! I apologize, repent, and ask for your forgiveness. I acknowledge that you are a good, good God. If there are any other gifts that have been given to me that I have misused or shut down, I repent for this and ask for your forgiveness. Please open my mind and my heart to search out the plans and mysteries you have for me. May I ALWAYS come to you for guidance if I do not understand something or if I need your revelation. Thank you, Jesus, for my salvation that was paid for on the cross. Your love overwhelms me. Amen.

Excellent! Repentance breaks the weapons of the enemy. You did it! Your angel is doing a little jig of happiness. The next prayer is important, but I will put a slight warning label on it. It is the prayer to ask God to "flip the switch." After praying this prayer, the emotions often begin to come back full force, as if you just turned on a faucet. You may have a few days of intense feelings, but I do not want you to be afraid—God knows what you can handle!

With this new flow of emotions, two things will happen:

1. **You will begin to feel.** That is the assurance from God that He has now installed or turned on this

gift. Begin to thank Him and praise Him. It is
the assurance that you have stepped up a rung
on the ladder—you've received an upgrade.

2. **God will protect you.** If He is handing out a gift,
    you can be assured that He will shield you while
    you discover how to use it. But that means you
    have a responsibility to continually learn. I do
    not want you to be stuck in a state of not advanc-
    ing forward. Okay?

If you say this prayer and nothing tangible or noticeable happens,
don't worry! The shielding has likely already begun, and God will
peel you like an onion. In other words, there will be layers of discovery as you slowly unwrap your gift. Some layers will be revealed
with intensity and some with spiritual enlightenment—a moment
of revelation in the spiritual that becomes a reality in the physical.

PRAYER TO RECEIVE YOUR GIFT(S)

*Father, I have repented before your throne for the
gift(s) that I have rejected and shut down. I now
ask for these gifts to be returned to me. I ask for
these gifts to be washed by the Blood of the Lord,
Jesus Christ, and be redeemed and cleansed by the
Holy Spirit, especially if I have misused the gifts
you gave me. I also ask for the ability to learn and
manage these gifts. Please restart what has been
given to me. If any of my giftings have been dulled
by warfare, I ask for them to be sharpened and
ready to be used. I pray all of this in the Name of
Jesus Christ. Amen.*

Fantastic! My mama heart is beaming with pride at your coura-
geousness. Because of the flood of emotions that you may experience, be attentive to God's protection. If your gift becomes over-
whelming at first, just ask for God's protection. You need to believe
that this is part of the healing process.

If you experience intense negative feelings, pray! Pray for the
opposite feelings to manifest. Pray, be thankful, sing praises to the
Almighty, and/or listen to worship music. These are examples of
practical things you can do to combat negative feelings. Do not let
the enemy take back any territory. He just lost part of the hold he
had on you.

My dear friend Jenna Winston has a prayer that may be helpful
when it comes to breaking partnership with the enemy. In the above
prayers, you have repented for disposing of the gift, then you prayed
for the gift to be returned, and now this prayer is to break agreement
and partnership with the enemy that you may have inadvertently
participated in. We are taking care of anything that may have been
opened and closing all possible doors, in the general sense.

PRAYER TO BREAK PARTNERSHIP WITH THE ENEMY

> *In the Name of Jesus Christ, I break partnership*
> *with the enemy. I repent for any authority or part-*
> *nerships that I have made with the enemy, and I*
> *come to you, Lord, and ask that you close every*
> *door that is not of you and had access to my gift-*
> *ings. I ask that you completely cleanse my giftings*
> *and realign them with heaven, that I would only*
> *see and feel and understand what you want me to,*
> *in Jesus' Name. Amen.*

I can't help but have joy bubble up inside me at the thought that the enemy has lost territory. I have this urgency to bust out laughing. I am proud of you! Now, let's get started developing your feeler gift!

CHAPTER TWO

EVERY GOOD
AND
PERFECT GIFT

Is there such a thing as a "feeler" gift? Because this gift is not listed in the gifts that the apostles wrote about in the gospels, some people discount its validity. But for the ones who have been given the gift of a feeler, they absolutely know that they have feelings and emotions that they cannot account for.

My friend Andrea Nelson often shares her testimony of her feeler gift. Her whole life she has been considered an emotional person and was often told to "just get over your emotions." When Andrea shared with me, she said, "I would walk into a room and suddenly start to cry or be around certain people and become very angry. I had all these experiences, and I never knew what to do with them." When she began her first year at Bethel School of Ministry in 2004, the rollercoaster of emotions began again, and she thought she was a crazy person. "I thought I needed deliverance or lots of ministry time."

Chad, one of the third-year students at the ministry school, came up to her one day and said, "Andrea, you are a feeler, and you are sensing the atmosphere. You are not crazy, but you are actually encountering what God is doing in the room." He began to give her tools to use whenever she got the feeling of being overwhelmed. Andrea said that everything shifted for her once she had tools to navigate what she was feeling. One of those tools is accepting and understanding that your feelings are a gift from God!

What I have learned over the years is that not every gift that God gives is in the Bible. For some people, this sounds like heresy, and for others, they may think I will be struck by lightning at any moment. The truth is, the Holy Spirit can operate outside of the presumptions, parameters, or restrictions we have placed on Him. I can attest to this.

For many years, I put the Holy Spirit, and God, for that matter, into a box of my understanding and what others had taught me about Him. When we talk about the feeler gift, people want the biblical evidence to substantiate this gift. I totally get that. But for the ones that have this gift, how do you prove to others what you are "feeling?" It is difficult. Just like it is for the ones who smell a demonic presence. Yep, you read that correctly. There are those gifted with that ability. They can even smell the sweetness of God as His presence fills a room. There are also those who feel the presence of God on their skin when He is near or when they hear His truth. God is the One who created all our senses, and He has a use for each and every sense in the physical and spiritual realm.

AN ABUNDANCE OF GIFTS

Paul wrote about spiritual gifts in Romans 12. I have heard many sermons and lectures on this subject, but none that fully develop what I want to share here.

Paul wrote about seven gifts. In Romans 12:4-8 it says:

> *For just as each of us has one body with many*
> *members, and these members do not all have the*
> *same function, so in Christ we, though many, form*
> *one body, and each member belongs to all the oth-*
> *ers. We have different gifts, according to the grace*
> *given to each of us. If your gift is prophesying, then*
> *prophesy in accordance with your faith; if it is*
> *serving, then serve; if it is teaching, then teach; if*
> *it is to encourage, then give encouragement; if it*
> *is giving, then give generously; if it is to lead, do*
> *it diligently; if it is to show mercy, do it cheerfully.*

I contend that Paul has listed most of his own gifts as an exam-ple. This is *not* the ultimate recipe or list of gifts that people may have. In my distant past, I heard people give lessons/sermons about these gifts, that you are only allowed one, and you need to discover which one is yours. This is not true. Look at the list one more time. These are all Paul's own gifts, and he was giving an example of what to do with each one of these gifts. I can assure you that Paul learned what to do with each one of his gifts.

I find it interesting that Paul listed mercy as the last example. The Lord was teaching him mercy after Paul's encounter with Christ. Saul (who became Paul) was the vigilante who had no mercy on those who believed in Jesus. The word vigilante comes from the word vigilant. Saul was there to protect the cloaks of the ones who stoned and murdered Stephen, one of the disciples who was first martyred. Saul was a participant, even though he did not pick up a stone. And he became the hunter commissioned with destroying the new movement, with full permission and agreement from the Pharisee leadership.

When Saul had an encounter with the Lord Jesus Himself, this changed everything for him. The scales of his eyes were peeled off, spiritually and physically. Saul could clearly see what he was meant to do for the rest of his life. He learned mercy from Jesus, who gave him mercy. Even though Saul had an encounter with Jesus, he still needed help from Barnabas, who brought Saul to the apostles. Everyone was afraid of Saul and did not want him to join with the disciples, but the apostles needed to give Saul the stamp of approval. This encounter with Jesus made Saul fearless because he knew the truth and the apostles became convinced that Saul had an encounter with the Lord.

In Romans 12, Paul wrote about the different functions of the body, which He related to the giftings. Paul did not list every function of the body. Just because Paul does not list these different functions does not mean they do not exist. Paul wrote about the gifts in 1 Corinthians 12:4-6, as well: "There are different kinds of gifts, but the same Spirit distributes them. There are different kinds of service, but the same Lord. There are different kinds of working, but in all of them and in everyone it is the same God at work."

Paul proceeded to list out some of the "manifestations of the Spirit" from verse 7 through verse 11. These are examples of the Holy Spirit's gifts and manifestations, but it is not a comprehensive list. Paul did not list the services that the Lord extends or the different kinds of workings. As a side note, the people that Paul wrote to were the Greeks in Corinth. They had a god for each gift and for every job. They had many gods. The point that Paul wanted to make was that there was One God, not many.

Do you notice that Paul used the words, "same Spirit, the same Lord, and the same God"? He wanted to impress upon the Corinthians that even though we use a different word, it is the same God that he is talking about. Paul also mentioned one body with many parts. He contended that it is important to understand the Oneness of God, even though there may be different facets of the Lord. And he uses the example of our bodies to prove his point.

Continuing in 1 Corinthians 12:12-19, we read:

> *Just as a body, though one, has many parts, but all its many parts form one body, so it is with Christ. For we were all baptized by one Spirit so as to form one body—whether Jews or Gentiles, slave or free—and we were all given the one Spirit to drink. Even so the body is not made up of one part but of many. Now if the foot should say, "Because I am not a hand, I do not belong to the body," it would not for that reason stop being part of the body. And if the ear should say, "Because I am not an eye, I do not belong to the body," it would not for that reason stop being part of the body. If the whole body were an eye, where would the sense of hearing be? If the whole body were an ear, where would the sense of smell be? But in fact God has placed the parts in the body, every one of them, just as he wanted them to be. If they were all one part, where would the body be?*

God uses every one of our parts for His glory. He will use the eyes of the seers to see into the spiritual realm and the ears of the hearers who hear from God. And He uses the feelers to show that God is a God of emotions. He is a God that gets to the heart of things and shows Himself as approachable.

THE GIFTS ARE IRREVOCABLE

In Romans 11:29, the Apostle Paul writes, "For God's gifts and his call are irrevocable." The dictionary states that the word irrevocable means to not be able to change, reverse, or be recovered; final. Something that is irrevocable cannot be undone or canceled.

No one can cancel your gifts, not even you. God desires to pour out His Spirit and gifts on us all, who are we to limit Him or His expression of gifts? We have no concept of the extravagance and generosity of God, and of His imagination of gift and tool giving. His storehouse is huge! I have realized that I cannot put a limit on God, and neither should you. He has busted out of the box I put Him into. He is the super, super, superhero of box busting!

Solomon said, "But will God really dwell on earth? The heavens, even the highest heaven, cannot contain you. How much less this temple I have built!" (1 Kings 8:27). Solomon knew that God could not be contained even in the highest of heaven. How can we regulate God into a place or a box? He operates without the restraints of time itself. Why? Because He was the One that created time.

Who are we to tell God how to distribute His gifts? The clay cannot tell the potter how to operate His wheel or what vessel to create. Just like when Jesus was asked when the Kingdom of God was coming (Luke 17:20-21), He replied, "The coming of the kingdom of God is not something that can be observed, nor will people say, 'Here it is,' or 'There it is,' because the kingdom of God is in your midst."

That was a radical way of thinking for the Pharisees who were asking the question. And it was just like Jesus to pop the bubble of their way of thinking. Jesus can also pop our way of thinking about how or why He distributes gifts. For God is a kind Father who loves giving out gifts. It is one of His love languages.

EMBRACING THE FEELER GIFT

It is difficult for feelers who have been discounted in what they are feeling and experiencing to be told this "emotion stuff" is a gift. I am sure that there are many feelers out there who have been told that they are too emotional. Others may have been told to "get a grip on yourself."

Navigating other people's responses to you can be difficult, but so is managing your own self-criticism. For example, berating yourself when you begin feeling other people's emotions. Someone starts crying and you participate with buckets of your own tears. "Get a grip!" you think to yourself. Another example is when you walk into a building and feel foreboding or calamity. Or you walk around inside a store and begin to have thoughts that are usually not your own. These emotions sometimes spring up suddenly and we get caught off guard. That, however, doesn't mean this isn't a gift worth embracing!

Before I knew about the feeler gift, I remember walking into a room and suddenly stopping and literally backing out of the room. I did not know why, but I felt an evil presence in the room. There were other times that I would stay out of a room I was supposed to enter because of a foreboding feeling. I would then take a deep breath and say a prayer, "God help me," before entering the room. As I began recognizing the feelings as part of my gifting, that prayer was just enough to give me relief to cope with those feelings.

For the beginning feeler, it does take practice and requires that you pay attention. If you have said the prayer to turn on your feeler gift, it can be a little messy at first until you get some tools in your belt. If the atmosphere is too chaotic, then walk away for a moment. Take a deep breath, ask the Lord for strength, and see if you can go back into the environment. The Lord has given you this gift and you are learning about yourself and the atmosphere around you. Think of yourself like a great explorer, a modern-day pioneer. Every pioneer is a little nervous about the unknown, but they press on. God abides in you; therefore, you are bigger than the atmosphere. But this is also a discovery of yourself. You must be vulnerable before God and begin to understand the feelings He is asking you to deal with. We do this as we develop our relationship with Him and know our identity that He has given us.

One of my good friends, Barbara, was shopping to buy a used car with low milage. She and her husband, David, knew what they wanted. As they went to the first dealership, they found the exact car that she wanted, but she did not feel like they should buy it. The idea of owning that car made her uncomfortable, even though it had everything on their list. They went to another dealership and found almost the exact car, and she fell in love with it. It was perfect. Why? There may be several reasons. Barbara is in tune to her feeler gift. It comes naturally because she walks closely with God. Was the discomfort of the first car because God was telling her that there was something wrong with the car? Or was it because there was a "residue" left from the previous owner? She did not stop to analyze. She simply trusted her feelings and continued on until God said it was right.

Embracing your feeler gift is challenging, especially if you've had negative experiences in the past associated with the things you feel. I have not read in the Bible that a prophet walked into a building and felt disgusted, anxious, or fearful for no reason. But there are people that are experiencing this. How do you explain this? God has given us the ability to discern people's emotions. Not only that, but by our feelings, we are learning to discern what God is trying to tell us. Understanding our own feelings verses what the feeler gift is trying to reveal to us can seem like walking a tight rope. With a little practice, however, and a daily walk with God, embracing the feeler gift becomes a joy and not a struggle.

IT STARTS WITH RELATIONSHIP

Ephesians 2:8-10 says, "For it is by grace you have been saved, through faith—and this not from yourselves, it is the gift of God— not by works, so that no one can boast. For we are God's handiwork, created in Christ Jesus to do good works, which God prepared in advance for us to do."

I love the fact that God has given us gifts because we are God's handiwork. We are His creation, uniquely built, and we have our own DNA that no one else has. Think of the complexity of how we are born and the fact that we are so distinctive, to the point of having our own fingerprints and our own DNA. This signals to everyone else in the world that we are individually made by God. You are special and brilliantly created.

Along with being God's individual creation, we were made to do His good works. We are in partnership with God. He is relying on us to do His works that He prepared in advance for us to do. Gadzooks! And I can personally testify that I have failed in this mission. There have been instances that I have failed and gone in a different direction that God wished me to go. I bet there are plenty of us that can raise their hands up and say, "me too." And that is what is so awesome about God: He provides mercy and forgiveness. His love for His children says, "Let us try this again."

We may have missed opportunities because we decided to go in a different direction, but I can assure you that God has more good works for us to do! He desires us to be used by Him. Do not let guilt and shame be planted into your soul because you think you have "failed." Repent, forgive yourself, shift into another mindset, and go on. To repent means to turn around into another direction. It is that easy!

When my children were small and just learning to walk, they would crawl then, eventually, stand. They would hold onto a table for dear life to steady themselves. We, as parents, would stand back and grin, knowing that they were strengthening their legs and backs by the simple task of them standing. Eventually, they would let go and try tottering off on their own. They usually did not get very far before they would crumble to the floor. I would run over, pick them up, dust them off, give them a kiss on the forehead, and encourage them to try again. This is exactly what the Lord does to us. In our partnership with God, we have crumbled and fallen. He under-stands that we are learning and strengthening ourselves. "Alright, my dear one, let's try this again," He says.

I want to assure you that we are not working our way into the Kingdom. We are saved by the grace of God, not by our works. But we are co-workers with God, not having to work our way into His good graces but working alongside Him and His parameters. We are given grace to learn, grow, and co-labor with Him. It is a loving relationship that we are partaking in. Just like in a marriage, we love doing things for our spouses, and we do not have to "work" ourselves into experiencing their love. It is this heart position that the Father loves. How do we position our heart towards Him? Love and humility are of the greatest value to the Lord. He can then use you in magnificent ways. He chose you for His great works. And just like any good parent, He loves to see your growth.

John 15:14-17 says, "You are my friends if you do what I command. I no longer call you servants, because a servant does not know his master's business. Instead, I have called you friends, for everything that I learned from my Father I have made known to you. You did not choose me, but I chose you and appointed you so that you might go and bear fruit—fruit that will last—and so that whatever you ask in my name the Father will give you. This is my command: Love each other."

A friend helps out another friend. It is a bond that is developed. It is a partnership of trust and love where we rely upon each other. We are not called to work for God, but we are called to love God with everything that is within us and co-labor with Him. "Hear, O Israel: The Lord our God, the Lord is one. Love the Lord your God with all your heart and with all your soul and with all your strength" (Deuteronomy 6:4-5). Instead of "O Israel," I always put my own name in that verse. This is my proclamation to the Lord. I love You my Lord with everything that I have within me.

I went to the Catholic church while growing up and then to conservative Evangelical Christian churches in my 30s. God is always good about revealing Himself through the Scriptures. I knew about God, but I didn't KNOW Him. There was a time that I walked away from God and came back to get reacquainted. But it was not until I gave my "yes" to the Holy Spirit in my late 50s that things began to change rapidly for me.

My first manifestation that I experienced in the Spirit was tears. I knew He was there when tears would begin to form inside my eyes without any reason; they would just come. I would begin to feel the wonderment of His Presence. I sensed that it was also a washing away of any preconceived ideas I had of Him. There would be days when I would cry all day long, dabbing my eyes with tissues as I tried to function throughout the day. It was an interesting and hilarious time in my life. I would yearn for more of God, but when He showed up differently than I expected, I would say, "Whoa now" as though I could try to regulate Him. He wore me down. After trying many times to regulate His functions, I just gave up and laughed at my own inability to function in a dignified way.

I began to lean into knowing God and having a fresh and new relationship with Him. And in response to my growing relationship, God began to reveal Himself to me. He unveiled mysteries and revelations. The Scriptures came alive, and I had a thirst for His knowledge that could not be quenched. And let me tell you a secret about God, He is quite the character, and He is hilarious! I encourage you to give your "yes" to God and surrender yourself to Him. The journey is amazing and thrilling.

Are you ready and willing to give up to function in a dignified way? I am not talking about being irreverent. I am not talking about acting out and becoming a loon (definition of a loon is a silly or foolish person). What I am talking about is, if the Lord decides to manifest in a way that is awkward, would that be okay with you? God is not a disruptive God, but He does make things vulnerable. If there is pride attached to your anti-function, He seems to root that out. He brings things to the surface, like dross.

Dross is the process of making silver pure. In the olden days, silver was heated to a boil and the scum that came to the surface was skimmed off and tossed away. Then they would boil it again, and skim off the dross. They would do this several times to make the silver purer. The dross in the latter process may be saved to make a cheaper kind of silver, but the silver that was pure had no more dross to boil to the top. You would then be able to gaze into the pot of hot silver and see your reflection.

We all have dross in our lives. And when God is done getting rid of all our own dross in the process of growing, pruning, and molding, He will only see His reflection in us, and we will only see Him. And it all starts with relationship.

More than anything, God wants to have a relationship with us. We are precious to Him. We are cherished. What a lovely thought and a reality. Chris Cruz, the author of the book, *The Practice of Being with Jesus*, says: "God has committed to being more than a gift-giver. He is not content with simply blessing us. He wanted to give of Himself. The great goal of our life is to love God. We cannot find a better purpose." Jesus has the intense emotion of love towards us. And when He loves someone as much as He loves you, He can't help but give good gifts. How can we not help but love Him in return for all He has done for us?

EVERY GOOD GIFT

If you have been walking with a feeler gift, even if you didn't realize that's what it was, I can imagine that you have been frustrated trying to manage it. This gift is one of the main gifts that the enemy has misused against us. All gifts can be misused by the enemy, the devil. But the emotions that are attached to the feeler gift can be twisted and used against us. It is time that we take back the power and authority that God has originally designed us to have.

I understand the frustration you may have with this gift—the emotional breakdowns concerning it, and also the misunderstandings you have had to deal with it. But, because it is given by the Gift Giver, even though we do not understand it, that does not mean it is not good. Believe me when I say it is a good gift, despite what you "feel" about it (a little feeler joke).

As we previously read, James 1:17 says, "Every good gift and every perfect gift is from above, coming down from the Father of heavenly lights, who does not change like shifting shadows." The feeler gift is a gift from God. It is good and it is perfect because it comes from Him.

You are one of the anointed that have it. I think it is about time that you begin to learn about this gift and how to manage it. Then you can rule the world! Just kidding with that one. But you will be able to change the atmosphere because you will be dealing with the spiritual realm. How exciting is that!

Ever since that first visit to the Oregon Country Fair, I've grown exponentially in my understanding of the feeler gift and how God speaks to me through my emotions. At the fair, for example, He was making me aware of an atmosphere that was both spiritually open and spiritually oppressed. I knew enough at that point to understand that feelers who feel certain things in the atmosphere or within their sphere of influence have been given authority over that particular sphere.

While I didn't have authority over the entire fair, I had authority to change the atmosphere around me. It was likely that authority, released as I prayed for the dancers, that attracted the attention— and the curses—of the man dressed as a warlock!

Because God anoints you and I differently, your experiences with God and His gifts will be different than mine, and even different than your neighbor's. I love how uniquely and individualized God installs our connection with Him and how we are used for His design and plans. Through sharing my experiences and those of my friends, you will see how differently God interacts with each of us—but you will also begin to identify common themes and ways in which the Lord speaks. You'll start to recognize and understand your own experiences and gifting by hearing, observing, and learning from others.

The feeler gift isn't only a good and perfect gift, it is a tool that God gave you to help with His works in the Kingdom. You were born with a tool belt. You had gifts already installed in the belt as you came out of your mother's womb and some tools are given to you when they are needed throughout your life. God does not direct us to a task without the correct tools or gift. It may be for a season that we are walking through, for direction on our path, or to fulfill our life's calling.

I don't believe the tools will ever leave your tool belt. The Lord uses all things that He gives you and sometimes "upgrades" your original tool for a better, more useful one, one that is sharper. It all depends upon your walk with the Lord. The more intimate the walk, the more powerfully He will use you.

Throughout the remaining chapters, we'll discuss how to identify and use this tool, how it often manifests, and practical ways to grow in your feeler gift. My goal is that you will gain a firm understanding of the feeler gift and how God can use you and speak to you through your emotions. Not only that, but I pray you experience an upgrade in your gifting and in the depth of your relationship with God.

CHAPTER THREE

HEARING GOD'S VOICE

"Why, oh, why do I have this gift? What use can it possibly be for?" These are some of the questions that I have asked the Lord. The better question I should have asked the Lord is, how do I manage this gift? This is a gift that needs to be taken care of, managed, sometimes controlled, and eventually loved. For beginning feelers, love may not be the word you would use to describe your gift! It is difficult to manage this gift in the beginning, but it can be done.

The more we learn about the feeler gift, the more questions emerge; and the best place to take our questions is to the Lord. Not only that, but the goal of developing the feeler gift is to recognize what God is saying to you and to others. It all comes down to communication with God. This is your first mission as a feeler: to hear His voice.

BUILDING A RELATIONSHIP WITH GOD

Let us go back to the basic foundations again. One of the foundations we discussed in chapter one is that we must be born again. Another is that we must develop a relationship with God. Having a relationship with God means interacting with Him. Talk to Him every day and as frequently as He comes to your mind. Remember, you are developing a friendship with Him, and to become best friends, you need to get to know Him. To know Him, you must engage with Him through the Scriptures and communicate with Him, just like you would any other friend.

Speaker and author, Graham Cooke, once said: "Change your relationship with Jesus from a visitation relationship to a habitational relationship." Our relationship with God needs to shift from an Old Testament understanding of a "visitation" from God to a New Testament understanding of habitation. He abides in us. Hearing His voice and communicating with Him doesn't need to be difficult—He is always with us!

If you are fairly new to hearing God's voice, you are developing a relationship with Him. And just like any friendship that is developing, it comes in stages. If you expect a person that is an acquaintance to give you intimate information about himself, that is not going to happen. It is a relationship that is developing. It takes time as you develop trust with this friend. I can tell you one thing, God is excellent with trust. He is trustworthy. It is usually us that breaks the trust issue. Either we decide to break off the communication we are having with Him, or we decide to take control of situations and venture off into the wild blue yonder without Him.

If you have struggled to hear God's voice, I have a prayer that helped me engage with the Lord and open up to hear from Him.

THE PRAYER TO HEAR GOD'S VOICE

Dear Heavenly Father, in the Name of Jesus Christ of Nazareth, who did come in the flesh, I ask that every part of my being would be led by the Holy

Spirit. I trust you, Lord, and I declare that I will hear the voice of your Holy Spirit and no other spirit will be allowed to speak to, or through, my heart or mind. Lord, I know that you lovingly created my spirit, heart, soul, and mind, but at this moment I want to hear from you. Therefore, Lord, I declare that my heart and soul will be silenced in a way that they will not be able to interfere with, influence, or corrupt the thoughts coming to my mind from you. Instead, I choose to entrust all my thoughts, feelings, emotions, desires, opinions, and imaginations to you, and I believe, and I declare, that I will hear your voice clearly and your truth will be revealed to me. Lord, I intentionally turn my mind and spirit toward you. Amen.

This is a prayer you can say before you do your devotions or when you need a specific answer from God. This is not a prayer you say once, and you will forever hear from God. But this is a prayer that may be helpful to open the gateway of communication as you build your relationship with the Lord.

EXCHANGING LIES FOR TRUTH

As you develop your communication and encounters with the Lord, you are also opening up your mind and your heart to a new way of dealing with your spirit. It's called putting on the mind of Christ. It works by doing an exchange with the Lord: His mindsets for your old ones. This is a conscious exchange that you do in your devotions. God gives you a new way of thinking (we call that revelation) and you deliberately decide whether to accept or decline this revelation. If you accept, you begin to see yourself, and the people or environment around you, differently. You begin to see things from God's perspective.

If this revelation (or the way you see yourself) is declined, however, then you may end up stuck in old habits and mindsets. It is sometimes hard to give up a belief (or emotions, traditions, or thought patterns) that you have held onto for some time. You believe it is real so you cannot give it to the Lord.

Lies that we have been given by the enemy (and have swallowed) are one way that the enemy has tried to keep us separated from the Lord. Just to be clear, the enemy is constantly giving us distorted information or lies. He may even sprinkle the information with a bit of truth, but overall, it is a distortion. Look, for example, at how Satan tempted Jesus in the desert.

In the book of Matthew, chapter 4, and also in the book of Luke, chapter 4, the Apostles tell the story of Jesus' temptations with the devil. Jesus was full of the Holy Spirit (Luke 4:1) and went into the desert where He fasted and was tempted for forty days by the devil. Luke says that Jesus was tempted every day, for forty days. It does not say how Jesus was tempted during each day, but at the end of the forty days, the tempter (the devil) came to Jesus and declared some distortions of the truth. And to clarify, the devil can, and will, use Scripture to distort his temptations.

The basis of the devil's temptations was to sow the seed of doubt about Jesus Christ's identity. The devil used the word "if." "If you are the Son of God…" (Matthew 4:3), and then the devil would quote Scripture. And Jesus combated the temptation and defamation of His identity by quoting Scripture in return.

Once this battle had ended, Luke 4:13 says, "When the devil had finished all this tempting, he left him until an opportune time." If you believe that you have won one battle with the devil, be assured that another battle will come again. And again. But as you walk with Jesus, the battles will become fewer and fewer, but the enemy becomes sneakier.

The fantastic thing is, as you walk with Christ, you are able to detect these lies and assaults with the mind of Christ that has been nurtured within you. The feeler gift can come with its own set of problems that the enemy uses to distort your perspective. If your feelings have ruled over you and have been difficult to control, I declare this to stop in the name of Jesus. It is time to not only learn how to manage your emotions but learn how to hear the voice of God so that His truth far overpowers the lies that the enemy would tell you.

LEARNING TO RECOGNIZE GOD'S VOICE

The more time you spend with the Lord, the more familiar His voice becomes. The number one aspect of God's voice is that He is kind and uplifting. He is never shaming or accusing. One easy way to differentiate between His voice and the enemy is by this one truth: He is always kind. If you hear things that are condemning, shaming, or discouraging playing in your head, that is not from God!

When we talk to God, His answers will always line up with Scripture. Remember, He is not condemning, shaming, or unloving. He encourages and lets us know how He loves us. He may guide, instruct, correct, or give revelations, but He will always do this with love and kindness.

If you are a regular communicator with God and He has been

silent, do not fret. If He has not answered a question or concern on your heart, then you must go back to what He said previously. You may be repeating the question, but He will not repeat the answer that He already gave. Are you asking Him again so He will adjust His answer? If that is the case, you may need to re-evaluate your heart.

For my friend Jill Lewis, her intimacy with the Lord and recognition of His voice starts every morning. I am in awe of how the Lord interacts with her. She told me how she wakes up with the Lord every morning. When she shared this, I looked at her and my jaw dropped. Jill wrote down her experience so that I could tell you:

"My habit, often, when I wake up in the morning is to take a moment and ask where the Godhead is. I don't like to get out of bed without knowing they are close. As I come into awareness of their presence, I know Father God is on my left, His forehead is pressed against my temple as He continually speaks His thoughts about me into my ear. Then, I realize Jesus is where He always is, behind me with His arms firmly wrapped around me. 'I've got your back!' He whispers, with a twinkle in His eye. The Holy Spirit then wraps us all together, like He is Sbinding us."

I had to ask Jill what "Sbinding" was. I had never heard that expression. She says, "He is like saran wrap. Or the clear plastic wrap you use on dressers and other furniture when you move. Only sparkling. Wrapping the three of us together."

Be just like Him, and be filled by the Holy Spirit, putting on the mind of Christ, and getting to know God through the Scriptures. His voice will become clearer and clearer as you develop your relationship with Him.

CHAPTER FOUR

INTERCESSION

If you, like me, ask yourself *why* you have this gift, it is because God believes that you are powerful enough to handle it. God has entrusted you with this amazing, multidimensional gift for a specific reason—and it goes beyond simply feeling what is happening around you. The feeler gift is also a call to intercession.

One of the main reasons that you have the feeler gift is because you are also an intercessor. An intercessor is a person who intervenes on behalf of another; someone who stands in the gap through prayer. Your prayers are powerful! That is one reason the enemy has tried to stop you from accessing your gift or tries to affect you by twisting your emotions.

The greatest intercessor of them all is Jesus and the Holy Spirit. He intercedes for us. In Hebrews 7:25, it states that Jesus is our intercessor. "Therefore, he is able to save completely those who come to God through him, because he always lives to intercede for them." Jesus is not only standing in the gap for our present identity (in Him), but also interceding for our future destiny.

Romans 8 is a revealing chapter (I highly recommend you read it), but more specifically for what it reveals about intercession. Romans 8:27 says, "And he who searches our hearts knows the mind of the Spirit, because the Spirit intercedes for God's people in accordance with the will of God." In The Passion Translation, the verse reads, "God, the searcher of the heart, knows fully our longings, yet he also understands the desires of the Spirit, because the Holy Spirit passionately pleads before God for us, his holy ones, in perfect harmony with God's plan and our destiny." When we are born again, we gain the Holy Spirit into our spirit. The more we engage with the Spirit and the mind of Christ, the more God's will becomes our will, and our will becomes His. We become like-minded. I love the thought that the "Searcher of Hearts" knows us so completely that His desire is to have us be in harmony with His plans.

From one intercessor to another, the prayers of an intercessor can change lives, situations, and even the atmosphere around you. Intercession is not boring or laboring. In fact, I have learned that it can be fun.

WHAT IS INTERCESSION?

First, intercession is all about going into the throne room of the Almighty. Wherever you are sitting, you are interacting with God, and you have been invited to walk into the throne room of God. This is a place where God gives you revelations and strategies. You walk into His war room. We walk into where He keeps treasures. When you become a best friend and a son/daughter of God, you are in a position to ask for anything. And like Solomon, I ask God for more wisdom. And I ask for more gifts. I have asked for the gift of increased faith. And as I write these words, I have been contending for the gifts of love and compassion. God exposes what we lack so that we can go to Him and ask Him to fix it. Like a child that has broken a toy, we go to our Father and ask Him to fix or transform things.

How you pray in your secret place of prayer will determine how you operate in the open. Your devotion to prayer will determine how you function within the boundary of the supernatural. You are developing a relationship and strategy with the Lord. He is developing a trust within you and for Him. You are allowed to peek inside His storehouse of treasures, mysteries, and wisdom.

When John the Baptist left the desert to engage with people, he had no confusion over his mission in life. People would come to him and ask him who he was. "I am the voice of one calling in the wilderness, 'Make straight the way of the Lord'" he would say (John 1:23). In his book *Rooted*, Banning Liebscher says it magnificently: "When God gives you this level of clarity about your part in His story and who you are, it brings great authority and focus to your life. Many people have no authority because they are confused as to who they are and what their role and assignment are in the story of God. God wants you to walk in so much authority and focus that you never waver from who you are."

As an intercessor, you have great authority. But He wants you to learn, develop, and use this gift, of being a feeler and an intercessor. It is your destiny to be in partnership with Jesus, standing in the gap. Begin to stretch the muscles of your mighty gift, by prayer, which is just talking to the Lord. I have used intercession to ask for healing, to prophesy, and to affect the atmosphere. I have asked for the Lord to transform people's hearts and to change situations. And interesting enough, to change the weather. I imagine a huge storehouse in heaven that I have access to, that is full of answers to prayer. I often imagine going up into heaven, sliding the gigantic door open, and looking at the answers that I need. It is like going shopping in God's mall. I ask to pull those answers down from heaven and install them into the people and situations that I am praying for.

Intercession opens the world to possibilities. As an intercessor, we are, in fact, duplicating what Christ is doing. He is standing in the gap of the present and the future. He stands with one foot in the present and another foot in the future, because time does not limit God. Through intercession, we partner with God to do what He does best: to change things. I am asking the Lord for things that He already wants for us. Why doesn't He just give it to us on His own? Because He desires us to co-labor with Him. We co-labor with Him to bring what is to come; to intercede and stand in the gap along with Him.

Paul talks about co-laboring with God in 1 Corinthians 3:7-9, "So neither the one who plants nor the one who waters is anything, but only God, who makes things grow. The one who plants and the one who waters have one purpose, and they will each be rewarded according to their own labor. For we are co-workers in God's service; you are God's field, God's building."

YOUR FEELINGS ARE A CALL TO INTERCESSION

I have a nurse friend who worked in the ICU at a large metropolitan hospital, and she has a powerful feeler gift. She was able to discern whether a patient's illness was attached to the demonic. She would just know that it was not a run of the mill illness, or it was generational. As she took care of her patients, she would pray and intercede the opposite of what she was feeling, and she would pray off any generational torment or harassment. She released peace into the room and blessed their family line, also praying for physical healing. She co-labored with the Holy Spirit on what needed to be prayed over each patient and would release and declare it into the room. She began to see incredible healing miracles. Her patients would recover faster than other patients and she would see a shift in many attitudes of the visitors when they came to visit. The things she felt over her patients were her call to intercede for them.

For many feelers, the call to intercession doesn't always happen on the job, but it happens in the middle of the night. I once heard a fantastic intercessor talk about the middle of the night time-frame. She said the spiritual atmosphere will be the most active from approximately 1:00 to 4:30 in the morning. From 1:00 to 2:30 or 3:00 in the morning is usually the demonic time and from 3:00 until 4:30 will be a time of the angelic and supernatural. Now, this is not set in stone, but I find this is generally true and interesting. The angelic does not set their watch alarms and when it dings, they say, "I'm on duty." However, I will often get woken up in the middle of the night to pray for people, places, family, and situations.

As I pray over what I feel and what I sense happening in the atmosphere, the time on the clock can be revealing. As I become alert, I check the time on the clock and get a sense of whether to do warfare or intercede for someone or a situation. I have a sense whether to interact with the angelic or do warfare over the demonic. The time on the clock is only a tool to be used, not a formula. As I am awakened, I listen to the Holy Spirit for instructions. It is like being sent on a mission. But instead of Mission Impossible, it is Mission Possible. All things are possible with God (Matthew 19:26).

As an intercessor and a feeler, it is time to pay attention to those moments when we are being called to intercede, whether at work, home, church, or even the middle of the night wake-up calls!

In April of 2016, there was a Christian stadium event in Los Angeles, California called Azusa Now. This was a huge event that Lou Engle orchestrated along with Bethel School and other churches in the area. I attended with the Bethel team, and one of our roles was to canvas L.A. and the surrounding areas to evangelize and invite people to the one-day event. I was a first-year student at Bethel (BSSM) and each group had been assigned a different area of the city. My group was assigned to the downtown/financial area. We were housed in a large hostel, that was older and had seen better days. It had marble floors as you entered the foyer and tapestries and Greek statues planted around the large entry area. My room-mate and I were assigned to a fourth-floor room, and we had the luxury of having our own toilet/shower in the room. Many of the rooms did not have that accommodation and the students had to walk down the hallway to use a communal restroom.

We had been warned of the rundown area we were going to be housed in; we were told not to venture outside after sunset. Our downtown area had many homeless that would set up their tents at night and then roll up their "house" in the morning. Their bathroom facilities were the gutters or light poles. Every morning, the businesses would hose off the stench and excrement from the sidewalks in front of their building as they rolled open their padlocked gates.

After a day of riding on a bus for eight to ten hours from our church in Northern California, we were all tired. We ate dinner and had meetings to discuss what we were doing the next day, and then we headed up to bed. The hostel was close to a fire station, so we experienced the sirens all night long as they sped away from their garage. My room looked out over an alley and the other side of the hostel faced a busy downtown street. The students spent much of their time looking out the windows at all the activity on the streets below. From midnight until the morning, we would hear screams, moaning, fights, and scuffles—not to mention the sirens. The next morning, the talk around the breakfast table was about the lack of sleep everyone had, the fearfulness of the atmosphere, and the noises that they heard all night long. We also talked about the nightmares that they were experiencing. I heard one student say, "We must have awakened most of the demons in the area with our presence." I thought, *this could be true!*

The next night, at approximately 3:30 a.m., I was awakened by the Lord. He told me to pray over the hallway and each one of the doors on my floor. I very quietly crept out of bed and walked the hallways and prayed over each door. There were doors where I felt the people in that room were having bad dreams and I would do warfare over those dreams. I broke atmospheres and asked the Lord to bring in peace, comfort, and good sleep. I walked the hallway for a little less than an hour and felt I was done, so I crept back into bed without waking my roommate. The next morning, the discussion around the breakfast table was about bad dreams that would start and suddenly end. Many students said that they had a peaceful and restful night.

That year at Bethel School of Supernatural Ministry, the Lord taught me many things about Himself, and He also broke the boxes that I had put Him into. I had many intimate encounters and experiences of wonderment with Him. I am in awe of the Lord and how He operates. It was not unusual for the Lord to wake me up in the middle of the night to pray. He did this often, but that time at Azusa Now was the first time that He gave me feedback on how my prayers affected the atmosphere. I really appreciated the confirmation that my intercession was affecting the atmosphere.

There will be days when you will have no idea how your prayers of intercession affect someone or someplace, but I assure you that they do. He does not wake you up or give you feelings just to disturb you. God has a purpose, and you may be the one to deliver what is needed through your prayers. You deliver blessings, break atmospheres, break the enemy's attacks, and deliver messages of love and attention.

CHAPTER FIVE
DISCERNMENT

Feelers don't always experience a feeling so that they can "fix" whatever is happening around them. Sometimes they experience or feel something simply to learn. God loves using our gifts to teach us who He is and what He is doing in and through us and others. How do we know when it's time to learn and when it is time to act? That comes down to utilizing discernment.

Discernment is a profound tool that we are all called to use, regardless of our other giftings. According to the Oxford Dictionary, discernment is, "The ability to judge well."[1] The definition that Wikipedia has for discernment is, "The ability to obtain sharp perceptions or to judge well… It involves going past the mere perception of something and making nuanced judgements about its properties or qualities."[2] Yet another source describes discernment as a way of judging between things, a perceptive view of things, and even a way to understand things that are often obscure or hidden.[3]

I love all these definitions as they help us understand this principle, but I also like to take it a step further. My definition of spiritual discernment is being so close to God's perception, that you begin

1   https://www.lexico.com/en/definition/discernment
2   https://en.wikipedia.org/wiki/Discernment
3   https://www.vocabulary.com/dictionary/discernment

to understand what He is telling you, without words. You become sensitive to God. You become acquainted with God's perspective of a situation.

Imagine being so close to God that you sense and share His perspective. Knowing Him in this way is mind-blowing—especially as you advance in your degree of discernment. Yes, there are levels of discernment, just like there are levels of knowing someone. As you get to know a person and hang around them, more is revealed about their personality, likes, dislikes, and experiences. That is the same with God. Hang around Him and get to know Him. Discernment is the foundation, the bedrock of all the gifts. The gifts of a seer, the feeler, the distinguishing of spirits, and prophecy, just to name a few. They all begin with the foundation of discernment.

DISCERNMENT AND THE FEELER GIFT

A good example of spiritual discernment and the feeler gift is in Mark 5:24-34. Jesus was on the way to Jairus' house and He was being pressed by the crowd around Him. There was a woman present who had been bleeding for twelve years. Despite many visits to doctors, nothing could resolve her issue.

To give you a quick history lesson, in Leviticus 15:19-30, we find instructions for a woman during her monthly flow. She is considered unclean. You cannot touch her, her bedding, or anything that she sits on. If you do touch anything that she has touched, then you are also considered unclean and must bathe, wash your clothes, and remain unclean until the evening. As for this dear woman, she had been in isolation and considered unclean for twelve years! The horrible situation in her body affected her ability to connect with God and her community.

This woman heard about the healing that Jesus could do and felt that if she could only touch Jesus' clothes, she would be healed. So, she came behind Jesus, and as He was passing by, touched the hem of His garment. Immediately her bleeding stopped, and she felt in her body that she was freed from her suffering. At once, Jesus realized that power had gone out from Him. He turned around in the crowd and asked, "Who touched my clothes?" (Mark 5:30). The disciples were confused; everyone was touching Him. But Jesus knew something was different. He felt something shift within Himself.

The woman was frightened and did not want to admit what she had done. Can you imagine what she must have been thinking? I am sure she believed that she had made Jesus unclean by touching Him. I would have been frightened too. But Jesus was insistent; He wanted to know who touched His clothes. Finally, the woman went and fell at Jesus' feet and admitted that it was she who touched Him. Jesus was not angry. "Daughter," He said, "your faith has healed you. Go in peace and be freed from your suffering" (Mark 5:34).

Jesus had discerned and felt the power that left Him at the woman's touch. That is amazing sensitivity. Jesus was so aware of Himself that He was aware when a "God-moment" took place.

Here is the point: we must become so sensitive, so discerning to the movement of God, that we recognize when a God-moment is happening. We must become so aware of our own spirit and soul that we recognize when something shifts. What does this look like practically? There are times when I can "feel" or sense when a more spiritually authoritative person is about to enter or has entered a room. And I can also feel the opposite, when a shift of the demonic happens.

DEVELOPING DISCERNMENT

It can take time to build this level of discernment. That is why there is no time like the present to get started! To grow in discernment alongside our feeler gift, we must become intentional in our relationship with God. As you learn, you will begin to discern what your spirit is sensing and how it is reacting when God's Spirit shifts things around you in the spiritual realm.

Begin to prompt yourself to look for something new or something that you have never noticed before in your everyday interactions with others. These observations will become easier as you are intentional to look for them. Be intentional to "feel" people around you: co-workers, people in the elevator, in the grocery aisle, sitting next to you in church. You may not feel anything, but then again, you may. Don't do anything for now, just simply pay attention. When you are intentional, God will help guide you. This is also creating muscle memory in your feeler gift.

For the beginning feeler, start paying attention to your environment. Ask God to help you. I also encourage you to write things down that you are experiencing. Carry a note pad with you and begin to write down your observations. It is easier to put things into perspective when you write them down.

As an exercise, write down how you are feeling in the morning when you get up. It is easy to write one or two words. Then, begin to notice any changes throughout the day. Put a time and place next to your words. If you can tolerate the constant note taking, do this for seven days. Make a note whether the weekend was a routine weekend, or you experienced a special activity on your days off. When you have a moment, after the seven days, sit down and ask God to reveal any patterns to you.

For many feelers, you may be able to see patterns of how your emotions are being dictated throughout the day. A pattern is similar feelings or emotions that surface in a certain time-period or a place. If the similarities are in a time-period, then begin to observe what is going on in your body during that time of day. For example, you are grouchy at 3:00 in the afternoon almost every day. That is a pattern. Lean into why that may happen. It could be the time of day that you are physically tired, and you begin to watch the clock for the workday to end. Or is it because your blood sugar levels have dropped and you need energy and a snack?

Lean into this "grouchy" feeling and pay attention. It may be that your feeling is connected to something else in the environment. Imagine yourself picking up the feeling like an object and examining it. Why is it familiar? Does it trigger me, or is it pleasant? Reach back in your memory bank for an example or duplication. Maybe your co-worker begins their work schedule at 3:00, the same time that you get grouchy. I am not saying your grouchiness is necessarily connected to your co-worker, but it is worth noting and observing the pattern. Ask the Lord questions about that co-worker. Are you reacting to something the co-worker is carrying? (We will talk more about this later). Is the feeling of tiredness from low energy or is there a spirit that lowers your energy that has entered the room? Begin to exercise your spiritual senses to the possibility of another spiritual entity in the room. This includes angelic activity along with the demonic.

As you open yourself up to "feel" and discern, you may find that some feelings become familiar to you. For example, there may be times where you meet someone and you instantly don't like them, or they irritate you. When this happens again, with a different person, that feeling of irritation or irrational dislike becomes familiar. You may be picking up on a "familiar spirit" that they carry, and it reminds you of someone else that carries that particular trait or even spiritual oppression.

While your first reaction is to draw away or be repulsed, our job as feelers is to reverse engineer those feelings to learn what God is revealing. Tap into that familiarity, or muscle memory, instead of avoiding it. This familiar feeling may have nothing to do with the person in front of you or the feeling in the room. Discernment will help you know when this familiar feeling is something that is triggering you, when it is a spirit, and how to respond to that person with love and openness despite what you feel on or near them.

FOLLOWING THE PATTERNS

Several years ago, I was a supervisor in Radiology in a large 450 bed hospital in Washington State. The hospital had a huge emergency room and surgery suites that operated 24/7. The activity that I had to manage during the day was tremendous. My wonderful staff of technologists had to be everywhere at once in the hospital. In my control area, I had a large white board (floor to ceiling) that I would use to write out all the exams for the day. This would include potential surgeries, exams that were scheduled, the different modalities that I had to coordinate with (MRI, CT, and Ultrasound), and the portable exams that were scheduled (not including the stats that were called in). There were days that I would have four "C-arms" going on in the surgery suites. (A C-arm is a portable X-ray unit that fluoroscopes your images into a live image. Many surgeries are done with a C-arm so that the surgeon can see that the pins he is inserting are correct or, in the case of gallbladder surgeries, he can see and image the contrast that is injected.)

At that time, I had a fairly new and young manager who wanted to make his mark on the department. He considered it his role to make the hospital money. Often, he would come into my area and examine my white board and decide to send one of my technologists home to make his numbers look good. Within an hour of him sending away one of my techs, I would be in desperate need of a technologist. Either an unscheduled surgery would develop or traumas in the emergency room would come in.

Whenever this manager came to my area, I began to eat crackers. I didn't know I was doing this until one of my co-workers pointed this out to me. It was enlightening to me. Why was I doing this? I figured out that I was stuffing my face because I didn't want to say anything to my manager out of disrespect. I realized that my cracker eating pattern occurred because I was feeling frustrated with my manager and loss of control over my own department. I was also irritated because I could see that he was only concerned with his own advancement.

I had learned from my past interactions with him that when I protested him sending someone home, it fell on deaf ears, and he would become angry with me. So, I kept my mouth busy with crackers. Eventually, however, the manager was disciplined by the director for running short-staffed during critical times. I was thankful that my emotional response to my manager hadn't caused me to behave in a way that impacted my job.

Pay attention to patterns. Be alert to your senses when you go to work, go into stores, interact with salesclerks, and observe and encounter other customers. Even in your day-to-day life, God is speaking to you through your feelings and your discernment.

EXPLORING THE SPIRITUAL REALM

Some people have a natural way of discerning situations or people. They have a keen sense of observation. For example, I am an observer. I notice a person's body movements and how their attitudes are expressed in non-verbal ways. This has been a lifetime hobby of mine, but what I didn't know, was that God was training me in my own discernment. Therefore, my hobby was my training. Now, when I observe situations or other people, not only do I observe what is going on in the natural, but I listen to what God is telling me—and what I'm feeling—in the spiritual. When you partner your spiritual discernment with the gifts that God has given you—whether it is seeing, hearing, or feeling (to name just a few)—then you can begin to understand what is happening in the spiritual realm.

Imagine your errands are a field trip, like when you were in school. Jot down your observations. Note any smells you experience, feelings that you sense, and observations you make. Interact with ALL your senses. Consciously bring them to the forefront of your mind and make your mind stand up and pay attention. While your mind is interacting with your senses, bring your spirit and soul forward to observe. (I hope I did not lose you just then.)

You are a triune being. There are so many things that God has made that have this theme of triune-ness. For example, the egg. It has a yoke, the egg white, and the shell. Another example is water. It can change its form to liquid, solid (frozen), and gas (vapor, like steam). Human beings are triune as well. We have a body, spirit, and soul. Each property of the human being has its own identity. They operate differently and ultimately God wishes for them to cooperate as one unit. We may spend a lifetime learning how to do this, but it is worth it.

There are instances when each one (spirit, soul, or body) will want to rebel or have authority over the other, and then there is chaos, confusion, or disorder. I'm sure each of us can attest to this phenomenon. When I was born again, my spirit became one with God Almighty. I did not "conquer" my spirit with this born-again experience, but instead my spirit came forward to feel and experience the spiritual realm in an unexplainable way. I was on the road to learning how to interact with God in a way that was beyond my understanding and greater than my existence. I felt different. I loved differently. And I wanted more.

Your soul, spirit, and body each have their own way of experiencing life and they sometime jostle for supremacy. You can almost feel the chaos as they jostle for position to be heard. Chaos may not be the right word, but you get the point. When I ask for my spirit to come forward, I am asking for my spirit to "rule" over my emotions, or my will. My spirit is one with God and I am expectant that my spirit will receive answers that are needed. When I ask my soul to come forward in any given situation, I am allowing my soul to use my God-given emotions.

I had the breath of God blown into my spirit and it became more alive. It was no longer barely alive, but it stood up, at attention. Imagine yourself being in grade school and having the teacher call out your name and say, "Pay attention, Barbara." You automatically shift your mind to be attentive. When I use the wording of stand up, or set myself at attention, this is the same thing. Spirit or soul, pay attention!

It is now time for your spirit and soul to stand at attention and begin to learn about the gifts and discernment you carry and what God has installed into your being. You are becoming an explorer in the spiritual realm.

CHAPTER SIX

INFLUENCING ATMOSPHERES

In my story about my manager in Radiology, I would begin to eat crackers so that I would keep my mouth busy and not say anything rude. There is more to that story. I began to go to the Lord about this man. I would get so frustrated, and my frustration would spill out in my devotions, and I would complain about him. The Lord said that I needed to bless him every day. What?! I did not want to bless him! I wanted to call down fire like the disciples when they were in Samaria. The disciples were rejected by the townspeople, therefore they wanted to call fire down from heaven to destroy them. Jesus turned to James and John and rebuked them (see Luke 9:51-55).

I may have grumbled about blessing this guy, but I obeyed the Lord. Every morning, before I got out of bed, I said a blessing over the manager. I prayed a short prayer that he would have a great day and as the days became a week or two, my prayers would get a little longer as I blessed him. After a few weeks, I noticed that he did not come into my area any longer. That piqued my curiosity. I went back to the Lord about this. God said that by blessing him every morning, it had opened up the atmosphere so that He could work on my manager without his knowledge. Light bulb moment! With intercession, you can change the atmosphere.

Besides the feeler gift being connected to the gift of intercession, another aspect of this gift is that you "feel" and shift the atmosphere. This takes practice and intent. Many of the feelings that you experience are not your own (another light bulb moment). You are actually feeling the atmosphere that you are standing in. Pay attention to this. Once you feel the atmosphere, you are able to partner with God to change it.

AN ATMOSPHERE SHIFT IN CHINA

My friend Erica, who was a missionary, would take friends and students on trips to Asia. They would go into the Asian countries on tourist visas. On this particular trip, this group of young adults landed in China in the afternoon, after flying approximately thirty hours. They were exhausted and jet lagged. The Chinese guides that were meeting the flight were so excited to show them their country, however, so they took them straight on a tour of the panda park directly from the airport. The group was only thinking of a soft bed. The group was almost delirious and exhausted from lack of sleep.

The culture of China is solemn and rigid and even within the panda park, people were reserved and respectful. Normally, when you are in a foreign country, it is not unusual to be stared at when you look different. Since so many people were looking at this group of foreigners, a bunch of the guys on the team began to wave and say exuberantly, "Hey" and "Hi, nice to meet you" to everyone they passed. The guys even began to high five the Chinese children. Suddenly, laughter began to break out everywhere they went. It was like something broke open in the atmosphere, and their group ended up having a prayer line at the entrance of the park. (Sometimes referred to as a "fire tunnel," this type of prayer line is when two sets of people line up opposite each other, and as people pass through the middle of the line, they are blessed and experience the Holy Spirit). As Erica put it, "It was amazing to see the atmosphere change when our group entered the park." Erica said that to see the Chinese people laughing and have such joy suddenly and not know why, was the most profound atmosphere shift she had ever experienced.

LEARNING TO FEEL ATMOSPHERES

One way to experiment with this aspect of the feeler gift is to practice. When you get out of bed in the morning, take a moment to assess how you are feeling. You may feel drowsy, for example, but I encourage you to press into the *emotions* you are feeling. As you leave your house, is there any change? As you are in the car (with your radio off), assess again your feelings or mood. Now, as you walk into the store, or the building you work in, stop and take a moment to assess the change in your feelings. Step out of your skin and intentionally "feel." There will be a change! Why? First, because you have turned on your gift through the prayer at the start of this book and you are beginning to feel. Second, because you are intentional to press into your feeler gift.

As you practice honing your ability to feel atmospheres, note the change of the atmosphere everywhere you go. Is it solemn? Tense? Lonely? Happy? Anxious? One question that you need to answer: did *you* drag any emotions of your own into that building? Be sure you are trying to feel other things, not your own stuff. Take a week or two to consistently practice these exercises. Whenever you change a physical location, stop, and assess your feelings. You are now engaging in the feeler Gift. You are leaning in and learning.

The next exercise is to pay attention when someone enters your space. When you are working alongside other people, lean into the change in the atmosphere. Is there a change? If so, how do your feelings change? Do your feelings change due to the fact you like or dislike that person? Write down the feelings you have around different individuals at that particular time frame. If you like or dislike that person, why? Use only one to two words to describe your emotions. Does the time of day make a difference when you feel that person? Use your feeler gift to intentionally feel the emotions or the soul of that person. The soul is where you carry your emotions.

Learning to feel atmospheres also requires you to tap into your other gifts of discernment and intercession. Understanding how the atmosphere changes when a specific person is around requires discernment of what the person is carrying. This takes massive practice and constant communication with the Holy Spirit. In fact, it is important to note that it is hard to verify if you are correct about what people carry. You simply cannot walk up to the person and ask if they have purity issues, or deal with depression. That would be awkward and awful. With the feeler gift, not only do you "feel" the emotions of others, but through practicing the things that you carry and noticing how they shift during the day, you also begin to feel an atmospheric shift when someone comes into your sphere, personal space, or metron.

A metron is the amount of physical space that you have around you that makes you feel comfortable. You can feel your metron being breached when someone stands too close to you during a conversation. You would naturally take a step back.

Someone has "invaded" your space. If that person steps forward to close the gap of your space, you naturally feel threatened or perturbed.

With the feeler gift, your metron is also your sphere of influence in the spiritual, and it can become much larger than your physical sphere. It can take on a spiritual area, and as you stretch your feeler gift, it can take on a whole room or even region. You may be able to intentionally feel the whole room, what it carries, and what is invading it. This all depends on the sphere of influence, or authority, that you carry.

As a believer, your sphere of influence is given to you by the Lord. This may be new verbiage for you. Another word to describe it would be authority. In this context of your gifting, God gives you authority over what you are feeling. This is why your feeler gift is so amazing. You have authority to intercede and change atmospheres. If you feel heaviness, you have the influence and authority to shift it into light. Most feelers want to avoid everyone or anything that feels dark or sinful. A lot of feelers will isolate or back away from situations. But we have authority over this sphere that is trying to influence us. This is one of those things that you must go to the Lord about. Talk to Him about your sphere of influence and how to grow in it. You do not want to take your weapon and go hacking away at the atmosphere unless you know what you are up against and have the authority to do so.

We are all in training. We are learning and probing with God. Remember that you are protected. If you come against something that is difficult or a sphere that you are not prepared for, send it back into the atmosphere (prayer regarding this is on the following pages). It is that easy! Then, ask the Lord to teach you. Examine it.

Let the Lord know that you are willing to learn. And be sure to be thankful to the Lord for all that you are learning.

CHECK YOURSELF AT THE DOOR

To review, in the previous chapters, we have talked about your intercessor gift and discernment. You are now leaning into feeling the atmosphere and emotions of other people. We have talked about stepping out of your skin and intentionally feeling the things around you. Dawna DeSilva, the director of the Bethel Transformation Center in Redding, California, lovingly uses the phrase, "check yourself at the door." You stop and assess yourself before and after you enter a new room or building. Is there a change? If so, what is it? Dawna has an amazing book (and audio message) called *Shifting Atmospheres*. It is a great resource for learning how to feel and change atmospheres beyond just your physical metron, and I highly recommend it.

When you check yourself at the door, you engage with the Holy Spirit and ask Him questions. This is the learning stage where He will begin to teach you. There are several questions that you need to ask:

1. What am I feeling? Pay attention to your different feelings and emotions.
2. Are these emotions mine? Is Holy Spirit trying to tell me something?
3. Are these feelings from someone else?
4. Are these feelings from the atmosphere around me?
5. Do I do anything about it (if it is coming from a person)? Or do I just pray? (Note: Always pray

but know that there are times the Lord is directing you to do something specifically or intercede
on a deeper level.)

There is a saying at Bethel church, "Don't be a thermometer, be
a thermostat." A thermometer is a device that takes the temperature
of the atmosphere, but a thermostat is a device that can change the
climate in the room. For the feeler, it is easy to intentionally feel the
negative atmospheres and emotions around you and be the thermometer. Yet, because you are the feeler, it is time to learn how to be
a thermostat: don't just diagnose the atmosphere, change it! How do
I do that, you ask? You lean into your intercession gift and pray. You
pray for the change. Regardless of what you feel in the atmosphere,
pray for the Kingdom attributes to manifest in that environment.

The enemy is constantly talking and using distractions. And
God is always communicating. What channel are you listening to?
Accessing your feeler gift is a bit like turning on a radio station. You
need to find the channel that God is communicating on. If you are
listening to the enemy's station (or only feeling/homing in on negative feelings), then you need to change the channel.

Sometimes we do not realize that we are on the enemy's channel.
How can we tell? Ask the Lord what He is feeling. If the feelings you
are experiencing are not what the Lord carries, then it is obviously
from the enemy. It is time to switch from thermometer mode into
being a thermostat by listening to the Lord. Does this sound like a
lot of work? It is at first. If the enemy has had you dialed into him for
a while, he may get upset when you start changing the channel on
him. Not to worry. You are under God's protection, and you need
to remind yourself and the enemy of that.

CHANGING THE ATMOSPHERE

One of the simplest examples of changing the atmosphere is walking into your church sanctuary. Remember, you have already assessed your own feelings before you came into the church. As I walk into the sanctuary of a church, I stop and stand next to the side of the door. First, I intentionally acknowledge God and His vastness. I praise His holy Name and begin to center myself into Him. This is a necessary practice—to be centered on and connected to the Lord. "Teach me, Lord," becomes my prayer. I then begin to assess and lean into what I am feeling, whether it is feelings within me or around me. Once I have centered myself in God, I can then feel if there is a difference in the atmosphere.

As you do this, use the example of the radio station, if that helps. Picture a radio in your mind. Feel what channel you are on. Now, reach up (in your mind) and begin to turn the channel. Turn the channel until you are connected to God, feeling the atmosphere you are standing in. What are you feeling?

At this point, I begin to go through the list of questions that I ask the Holy Spirit (for those that are just beginning this process, it is helpful to write these questions on an index card or on your phone). I have already assessed the feelings, then I ask:

1. Is the feeling mine? (Make sure that the enemy is not trying to have you partner with the current atmosphere, like he may have done in the past.)
2. Is it from someone else? (You could be near a person and are feeling them.)
3. Is this feeling in the atmosphere?

If, for example, the emotions that I am feeling are "unsettled and anxious," and I know from Holy Spirit that they are not my own or someone else's, then I know to pray into the atmosphere to begin changing it. Instead of partnering with the unsettled or anxious feeling, I pray the opposite words to counterattack those feelings. My prayer to the Holy Spirit and to the atmosphere would include words of peace, comfort, and love. I pray this under my breath: "I declare that the Lord will bless this sanctuary and that it will be filled with Your peace, Lord. That the people would feel comfort and that anxiousness can no longer be allowed to stay, in the Name of Jesus Christ. May the people feel love from others and especially Your love, Father. Amen."

Always pray the opposite emotion you are feeling and pray into the atmosphere one of the attributes of God. An attribute of God is one of His characteristics and part of His essence. An example of an attribute is: God is good, God is forgiving, God is all-powerful, God is kind, etc. God has so many attributes that it could fill up many pages. By speaking these out, you are reversing and taking authority over the atmosphere. Know God's attributes. This is part of His Name, which has all His power and authority.

This same practice can be used when you walk into a home or office building. What would happen if you partnered with God to shift the atmosphere at your workplace? Just as I prayed for my manager over the course of several weeks to shift the tension and atmosphere at the hospital, you can partner with God to influence your workplace environment. If you are not able to do this in an unobtrusive way at the door or when you first walk into work, excuse yourself to the restroom. It is a perfect place to flush any unwanted atmospheric feelings!

Jenna Winston, my lovely friend and former roommate, taught me a simple prayer many years ago to dispel what is going on in the atmosphere. I use this prayer all the time.

PRAYER TO DISPEL NEGATIVE ATMOSPHERES:

In the Name of Jesus Christ, I send back to the atmosphere what is not mine and break partnership with it. I take back from the atmosphere what is mine, washed by the Blood of Jesus Christ and cleansed by the Holy Spirit. Lord, I ask for your Presence to be here and I choose to be aware of you and only you. Amen

This prayer can also be used in hotel rooms, parties, funerals, family gatherings, or any gatherings where I need to dispel the negative things I am feeling and reconnect with God. It is interesting how the atmosphere will shift and feel better after I pray these words.

I will always say this prayer whenever I am in a hotel room. If I forget to say this simple prayer before I go to bed, I am reminded to do this when I am awakened in the middle of the night, either from a bad dream or something that is going on in the hotel room. "Oh yah, Lord, I forgot to bring in your Presence before I went to bed." And I say my prayer and promptly go back to sleep.

While I was in Riga, Latvia for Awakening Europe a few years ago, I was at a hotel next to the airport. My flight back to the USA was scheduled to depart early in the morning, and I thought the hotel was the best place to stay for my early departure. I went to bed extra early since I had to get up at 4:00 a.m. to get ready. And of course, I prayed before falling asleep. In the middle of the night,

I woke up suddenly, and I knew that the Lord woke me up for a reason. As I opened my eyes, I remember asking Him, why am I awake? I could hear lots of fluttering and squeaking just outside my window. I thought, I must have a bird nest just outside. I lay there, fully awake now, and wondering why I was awake. I got up, turned on the light and went over to the window to see what was going on.

As I peeled back the curtain to see, there in the fold of the curtain was a huge bat on my side of the window and open to the room. "Oh crap!" I thought. The body of the bat was approximately seven to eight inches long, with a wingspan of at least fourteen inches. It must have flown in through the window where it was open near the ceiling.

I backed away from the curtain and wondered what to do. I began to wonder if this was the only bat since I heard so many noises. I grabbed the phone with a shaky hand and called the reception desk. The lady at the front desk had very limited English. I tried to describe the bat in my room, and I finally used the word "bird," but she still did not understand. I insisted that I needed another room to go to, and she insisted she could not give me another room, that they were full. I put on a sweatshirt and went down to the reception desk to insist she come with me. She hesitated to come into my room, but eventually complied, and I went over to the curtain and moved it aside. She screamed when she saw the bat and suddenly a new room became available.

I quickly packed my bag as I kept one eye on the curtain. I thanked the Lord very mightily for waking me up so that I could take care of the situation. When we learn to partner our feeler gift with the Lord, He can help us recognize a shift in the atmosphere even as we sleep!

CO-LABORING WITH GOD AS A FEELER

Just like my experience with the bat in Latvia, the Lord will frequently wake me up to pray, intercede, or for me to become aware of a situation. Your feeler gift will be used in so many wonderful ways. I have been awakened in the middle of the night to pray for people, or I feel a situation in my neighborhood and begin to pray. In my travels, I have heard disturbances on the streets, and I start praying and then the disturbances dissipate. The Lord needs us to co-labor with Him. It is an honor and a privilege. You will begin to see things happen and change around you. It can be interesting and quite fun. And through it all, God protects you. I know that I have angels of protection around my house, because I have asked God for His protection and He has shown me His angels.

Of my list of questions to ask Holy Spirit in order to assess your feelings, there is one other question that I encourage you to ask: Is the enemy trying to use this emotion? We understand the enemy uses emotions and feelings against believers. But feelers are warriors. We war against the enemy. That is part of the intercession gift. We must suit up and be ready for battle. We are called!

When we walk into an area and feel an atmosphere that is not from the Lord, it can only be from the enemy, the demonic. So, in my sanctuary example, the feelings of anxiousness and being unsettled was the enemy's attack to disrupt the church service. Sometimes, when this happens, the feelers in the sanctuary who don't understand their giftings have a hard time with the atmosphere because the enemy is trying to cause chaos. So, instead of arming themselves for battle and shifting the atmosphere, they leave. When that happens, the enemy got what he wanted!

That is why it is extremely important for us to change the

atmosphere. Without intercession and co-laboring with the Lord, how are we going to counter the effects of the devil? As feelers, it is through discernment and intercession that we co-labor with God to shift the atmosphere.

I once talked to Jesus about this co-labor concept. Why does He, the God of the Universe, the Creator, need us to help Him out? "Jesus, you can do anything!" I said to Him. And of course, He can. Jesus told me three reasons why He wants us to partner with Him.

1. **The act of intimacy.** When you are working alongside someone, shoulder to shoulder, there is a shared motivation to complete the task and enjoy the results. We seek the satisfaction of hearing, "Well done!" We become friendly with our co-worker (Jesus), and we also become dependent on Him. It takes two, and God loves our dependency on Him. He loves our friendship. And He loves our relationship of intimacy and communication. It is an act of intimacy when we come into agreement with the heart of God, become one beating heart with Him, and hear His heartbeat for us, our community, our nation, and the world.

2. **The act of obedience.** God wants us to obey in order for Him to protect us and to grow us. He protects us from harm and grows us into a warrior and the loving partner that we should be. What would an army be like if there was no obedience, and everyone went off to do their

own thing? It would be a mess and chaotic. Warriors obey the Commander. He is the One that
sees the big picture. Obedience only feels hard
when we think we can run our lives better than
Jesus can.

3. **The act of participation with the Kingdom.**
How glorious is that! God loves to give us
"upgrades" in the spiritual. He loves to expand
our borders of learning, experiencing, and
depending on Him. His borders are extensive,
and we humans can never reach the edge of
His perimeters. He always has more to give, He
always has more for us to experience with Him:
more blessings, more provision, more of everything! We get to (I should say, we are allowed to)
participate in the more!

God wants us to be part of His solutions and part of His plans.
We become the mailman of His solutions, good works, and His love.
In other words, we are the Pez dispenser! The God dispenser for the
world. Kris Vallotton, in his book *Spirit Wars: Winning the Invisible Battle against Sin and the Enemy*, gives a great example of being
part of God's solutions. There was a time in Bethel's history when
witches would come to disrupt the service. Intercessors were doing
warfare constantly. Kris had finally had enough. He says in his book:

> *I decided to enact a new strategy. Whenever I dis-
> cerned that witches were present in our assembly,
> I would leave my seat and work my way over to*

where they were sitting. Then I would give each of them a big hug and tell them how much I loved them. They did not quite know what to do with a hug and a little love. It freaked them out. They were really fortified against rebukes and curses, but they had no defense for love. Over the next year or so, several of them received Christ, and the rest of them finally stopped coming to church. Love never fails.

This is an amazing example of being a God dispenser. God's love turned a negative to a positive by changing the atmosphere. Kris just happened to be the dispenser that God used.

God is a good God, and He wants us to learn and experience each step of His benevolence. We can't jump ahead and skip a step. Actually, we should not want to jump ahead and miss out on a step of His generous wisdom, knowledge, revelation, or gifts. I know I wouldn't! I want to savor each step at a time. It is like having the BEST meal of all times! I want to savor each bite, chewing it slowly as the flavors burst in my mouth. Each bite has a different flavor that expands in my mouth and tongue. Mmmmmm. I would want to keep eating without having my stomach get full. That is the joy of co-laboring with God, and the calling we carry as feelers.

WALKING IN AUTHORITY

In Luke 4:6-7, Satan tempted Jesus in the desert. He showed Jesus all the kingdoms of the world and said, "I will give you all their authority and splendor; for it has been given to me, and I can give it to anyone I want to. If you worship me, it will all be yours." Instead,

Jesus paid the price in full on the cross and took back the keys of authority that Adam gave away. While Jesus was on earth, and before He ascended into heaven, He gave those keys to us.

As children of God, when we become born again, we are given His power and authority. Matthew 10:1 says, "Jesus called his twelve disciples to him and gave them authority to drive out impure spirits and to heal every disease and sickness." In Matthew 28:18-20, when Jesus gave the great commission, He said, "All authority in heaven and on earth has been given to me. Therefore go and make disciples of all nations, baptizing them in the name of the Father and of the Son and of the Holy Spirit, and teaching them to obey everything I have commanded you. And surely I am with you always, to the very end of the age." This is a promise from Jesus.

When we walk in the power and authority that Jesus gave us, we can break the enemy's hold in the atmosphere. Therefore, when I walked into the sanctuary and felt the heaviness, I declared the opposite. I declared His light would be manifested in the sanctuary. When you encounter any spiritual entity that is not from Jesus, you have the authority to tell it to go in the Name of Jesus.

I have used a simple wording for these moments: I take off and put back on. I take off what the enemy is doing, and I put back on the Lord's blessing (or opposite emotion). Whatever you take off, you must put something back on as a replacement, something that is of the Lord, such as peace, comfort, or love. We do not want the enemy to have the opportunity to put back his own stuff!

When we feel things in the atmosphere that are also connected to a person, however, things can get a little tricky. As feelers, we can declare that any spiritual entity GO in the Name of Jesus and leave the atmosphere, but we should not declare an entity to leave any person. What we take off should be connected to the environment. Sometimes we will encounter people who have given the demonic permission to be there (on themselves) and we cannot change that fact when we are trying to change the atmosphere. What we can do is change the atmosphere of the demonic who are bothering others or the environment. Deliverance is the act of getting rid of the demonic from a person. Deliverance and changing the atmosphere are two different things.

Do you remember the Scripture in Luke 11:24-26? Jesus says, "When an impure spirit comes out of a person, it goes through arid places seeking rest and does not find it. Then it says, 'I will return to the house I left.' When it arrives, it finds the house swept clean and put in order. Then it goes and takes seven other spirits more wicked than itself, and they go in and live there. And the final condition of that person is worse than the first." The point Christ was making is that you do not want to cast out the demonic and not have the "house" filled by the Holy Spirit. A person needs to be in full agreement with their deliverance and they need to be willing to do the work of filling themselves up with the Spirit of God. Otherwise, that person would be in a world of hurt later. Therefore, it is important to first learn to walk in our authority over atmospheres and use our feeler gift to intercede for others. If you wish to learn more about deliverance, I encourage you to seek guidance from experienced members of your church.

So why is shifting atmospheres needed, even at church? People who are demonized usually do not realize the extent of the demonic influence or oppression in their lives. Most people in this situation get relief when they come to church, and they desire to be close to God. This is to counter the nay-sayers who believe that the demonic cannot be in church. It can, but it is a struggle for the demonic to be there. When someone's heart begins to heal or they break off lies from the enemy, they break off agreements with this demonic oppression. When you begin to fill your heart with God's purity, the gunk has to leave. As feelers, we can help create an environment where God's presence is welcome and watch as those around us receive freedom by encountering Him.

Atmospheres are where the spiritual realm hangs out. It is a multi-dimensional reality and place. There is so much activity happening in the spiritual realm that we are often unaware of. It would overload our senses if we had any concept of what was happening around us. We are never alone. As human beings, we are uniquely given authority in the atmosphere. Jesus gave us this authority. We cannot forget this. It is a massive responsibility that He is happy to share with us through co-laboring.

Changing atmospheres through our intercession should always be at the forefront of our minds and hearts. It is our role as feelers to pray, to declare, and to partner with God to change the atmosphere around us. Remember, we are meant to be thermostats. The good news is, we don't have to get it right all the time. God delights in us, even when we are clumsy with our attempt to help Him out. It reminds me of when my kids were young and wanted to help me with cooking. I remember the clumsy way they broke the eggs or dumped the flour in the bowl. It made a mess and I had to pick out pieces of eggshell from the bowl, but as a mom, I was delighted with their eagerness and way of helping. God delights in the way we are learning, discerning, and co-laboring with Him in our feeler gifts. Because we love Him. And He loves us. It is as simple as that.

CHAPTER SEVEN

FEELING THE EMOTIONS OF OTHERS

As I mentioned previously, a feeler has the ability to "feel" what other people feel or the burdens that they carry. When you sense the feelings of those around you, you enter another level of discernment. Most feelers have been dealing with this all their lives but may not have realized the extent of their ability. If that is you, it is likely you feel others' emotions and sometimes what they carry. For example, you can feel impurity, you feel people who make you uneasy, or you feel people's stress, anxiety, or their anger that they have tried to keep under control.

For many feelers, it is easy for us to feel the negative emotions coming from other people. I call it the garbage dump. It is like feelers are carrying this huge garbage can around with them and giving others permission to dump into it. People routinely come and dump their garbage (a.k.a. feelings) upon you, and you take it. Either because you are a good listener, you are compassionate and empathetic, or you have the desire to help (or so you have been told).

It is great for feelers to listen to other people and help them, but that does not mean we should take on their emotions. Sometimes we inadvertently absorb these emotions in order to relieve them of their pressure. My advice is to not do this. Your gift is not meant to become a burden in this way. Establishing boundaries with those around you is a good first step to preventing their emotions from influencing you. There is a great book I recommend called *Boundaries* by Dr. Henry Cloud and Dr. John Townsend, which provides practical tips about how to keep healthy boundaries with those around us. Another way to protect yourself from carrying unnecessary burdens is to shield yourself.

DISCERNING EMOTIONS

To discern or to feel other people is a great tool. It requires you to partner your discernment with your feeler gift as you ask yourself, what is theirs and what is mine? What are they feeling? This is a great way to partner with God to minister to people's hearts and desires through prophecy and prayer.

To develop this aspect of your gift, be intentional to "reach out" spiritually to discover what other people are carrying. I once went to a large superstore when I began to stretch this gifting. I was on another field trip, and I was there to discover and learn. As each new person passed by me, I would try to understand and ask God what they carried. I would stand and pretend to look at clothes or produce and sense the environment and what others were carrying.

One guy that walked by me stopped and began to look around, wondering what had just happened and what had interacted with his soul. It was as though I had invaded his spiritual bubble. The Lord started to instruct me that some people are more sensitive to the supernatural. I had disturbed his senses. He felt something draw his attention. That has only happened a few times and I find it interesting. I knew God was teaching me something and I wanted to pay attention. Talk to God about *everything* He is teaching you. There are no coincidences.

You can build this part of your gift by asking yourself a few repeat questions.

1. Is it mine? You may need to have a major discussion with the Lord about what you are experiencing. There have been a few times that I have run into people that I have had a disregard for, and I have no idea why. After examination, and help from a friend, I learned it was a familiar spirit that my ex-husband carried. I naturally had an aversion when I rubbed up against it. Once I recognized it, I could say to that particular spirit, "I see you and you cannot affect me any longer." I then could make an attempt to love that person and to bless them.

2. Is it theirs? Many times, that is affirmative. People have carried their burdens for so long that they are unaware of what they are carrying.

3. Holy Spirit, why are you showing me this? The Lord is showing you this for your information and to learn from it. He is preparing you for a time when you will need to pray it off of someone. The Lord is preparing the groundwork so that when it is time to act, you will be ready for the assignment that He has given you.

4. What exactly am I feeling? Examine what you are actually feeling. You know it is not your emotions because you have asked the Lord. This is the time to pray the reverse of those feelings you are experiencing. Put words to these emotions or feelings.

5. Is it attached to sin? Examine if this feeling is attached to sin. Many times, feelers feel the negative first and it is attached to something unpleasant in the spiritual realm. It can be sin that the other person has agreed with, or it can be sin that has been perpetrated against them and they are carrying the residue. It can also be generational sin that they may unaware of. The generational sin is a harder one to discern and it takes some practice and conversation with the Holy Spirit.

I understand that some of these questions may not be answered in a casual setting like a grocery store or a mall. But this is your training ground. You are discovering and examining your giftings.

As you learn about the feeler gift and begin to feel others' emotions, practice on people you know. This gives you access to ask questions. For example, ask your co-workers, friends, or family if they are experiencing the emotion that you are sensing from them. Be open to their honest feedback—that is the best way to grow and learn!

As beginning feelers, we are often able to pick up on strong emotions easier, and unfortunately, they are usually negative emotions.

Be sure to ask questions about other people's emotions with sensitivity and without intruding or using "Christian-ese" or unfamiliar lingo. But also, be ready for the explanations that may ensue. Being sensitive to what they are feeling sometimes means you just need to listen. Just because you feel an emotion correctly does not mean it is the time to solve their problems.

If I feel someone carrying depression, I will ask, "Are you feeling a little down today?" Or if I sense anger, I will say, "I have a sense that you are annoyed. Is there anything I can do to help? How about I buy you a cup of coffee or tea?" Positive emotions should also be recognized and acknowledged. Another conversation starter could be, "I feel a lot of peace from you. Do you ever have trouble keeping your peace here at work?"

Once the person responds or confirms the emotion, I may explain what I felt and offer to pray for them. People are usually receptive to prayer as it is a sign that you care. Many times, you may encounter people in an environment that is not conducive for prayer in that moment, but just having the reassurance that someone cares enough to act upon their needs is enough to give them peace.

Remember my friend Andrea Nelson (in Chapter Two) who used to think her emotions were an indication that she was crazy? Once Andrea had tools for navigating the atmosphere that she was feeling, the Lord gave her a new tool that she began to feel on her physical body. For example: whenever she felt a heaviness on her shoulders, she knew that there was oppression that was weighing upon the person's shoulders like a heavy weight. She could easily pray joy and peace and lift off that oppression.

Discerning the emotions of others can look and feel different for each one of us. Sometimes understanding what you are feeling takes time, practice, and communication with Holy Spirit. There have been times when I've been alerted to the fact that someone is angry, even before they enter the room. I could feel them. As I mentioned previously, I can also feel the atmosphere shift when a spiritually powerful person has entered the room. It is as though my spirit stands up and is alert or activated. My friend Chelsea had a similar experience. She shared with me about a time she was at an event waiting to hear John Paul Jackson, the founder of Streams Ministries and a well-known teacher and prophet. She had her eyes closed when she suddenly felt him enter the room. His very presence shifted the atmosphere in the room. She turned around and, sure enough, he had just walked in and was standing at the back entrance to the sanctuary. The best way I can describe this is that I (and other feelers) simply experience a "knowing." I know or feel in my spirit what took place without seeing it in the natural.

An authoritative person can shift the atmosphere that they walk in, like the parting of the Red Sea. The relationship of Christ in them expands and it becomes the dominating factor in the room. The Christ inside dominates instead of what is happening in the atmosphere. It boils down to an intimate relationship with Jesus. As Graham Cooke says, the relationship with Christ becomes a habitational relationship instead of a visitational one. If you are going to Jesus like a slot machine, that is called a visitational relationship. You put a quarter in the vending machine and out pops your prayer request. But relationship with Christ does not work that way. The Lord wants an intimate relationship with us above all else, even our giftings.

When it comes to feeling the demonic activity on a person or in a room, some feelers describe a physical reaction, such as their skin crawling, a metallic taste in their mouths, or even a smell. Others simply feel the heaviness of the demonic presence in their spirits. Again, it is similar to knowing something without actually seeing or experiencing it in the natural.

I can also often sense when something is about to happen, and I begin to look around or "reach out" spiritually and try to find out what is happening or what people around me are feeling. My metron becomes activated and I can sense the good, bad, and ugly, as the Clint Eastwood movie would say. It is as though my metron expands and senses a shift that is happening.

There are so many ways to feel and discern the emotions of those around you. As I mentioned previously, the safest place to practice this part of your feeler gift is around people you can trust to give you honest feedback. But whatever you do, I encourage you to practice! The better acquainted you become with your ability to feel others' emotions, the easier it is to separate your own feelings from those in the atmosphere around you.

SHIELDING

To "shield" oneself is to intentionally not take on any emotions or feelings from another. This allows you to partner with God to use your feeler gift without becoming overburdened with what you are feeling. Shielding is like a protection barrier that filters unwanted or unneeded atmospheres and emotions. It will help you navigate through atmospheres without taking on everything you are feeling. It does not filter everything, but it reduces the intensity. It takes a lot of practice and there will be a lot of failures along the way, but that is okay! It is part of developing this beautiful gift.

I did not realize it at the time, but the Lord was teaching me to shield myself while I worked at the hospital. I saw quite a few traumatic things during my time there, but even in the midst of trauma, I still had to function and do my job. If I stopped and cried every time there was a trauma, or a child was hurt, I would never have gotten my job done. To be able to get my job done efficiently, I developed a way to shield myself or put those emotions up on a shelf until I was in a position to deal with them. Many times, I was on my way home from work, and I would cry like a baby. Or I would sense that I needed a break after a trauma scene, or I could sense that my co-workers needed a break.

A shield is a type of protection that you put over yourself from head to toe. Imagine a huge plexiglass container sliding over you. You can still see and interact with the world around you, but you are protected from anything infiltrating your shield. I would use this example in my imagination to shield myself at work. If I had to walk into a situation full of blood and guts, I would stop and initiate this protection. When I was just learning this technique, I would reach up and touch the side of my head, as though I was pushing my shielding button to initiate the shielding process. It is the act of being intentional with the shielding process. In the spiritual realm, it makes a difference when we are intentional. That is why, when we are dealing with the demonic, we say our prayers out loud. We are doing warfare and affecting the atmosphere with our words. I no longer work in a hospital setting, but I still shield myself frequently, depending upon the situation, and I do this automatically if the reason arises, especially with my feeler gift. In the previous section, I talked about expanding my spirit or my metron to feel what is going on around me. This cannot be done if I have my shield up. The shield limits me from "reaching out" with my spirit.

One of my friends, Andrea, is a trauma nurse who also works in the NICU (neonatal intensive care unit). She shared that her shielding mechanism is to use her imagination of a large zipper that she walks into and zips shut. This allows her to take care of babies in critical condition, comfort parents, and deal with life-threatening situations without becoming overburdened by the emotions or trauma around her. As a feeler, this is critical.

While part of shielding is to protect yourself from the atmosphere around you, or from taking on the emotions of others, it can also prevent others from "feeling" you in the spirit. At Bethel, for example, the public can make an appointment for a prophetic word. I am often on the teams that pray and prophesy, but I had never made an appointment for myself, and I wanted to experience it. So, I intentionally made an appointment for a zoom call with the student prophetic group (I knew that they would not recognize me).

As the session started, they explained the process of the prophetic word and stated that the two of them would go before the Lord to ask what He had to say to me. I waited for the word to begin. The minutes ticked by, and I was becoming uncomfortable. Usually, you hear from the Lord fairly quickly, but when it reached almost five minutes without them starting the word, I became concerned. Then the Lord very quietly said to me, "Put your shielding down." Almost immediately, they began their prophetic word. Another lesson learned!

Shielding allows you to protect your spirit while still staying connected with the Holy Spirit. I recently had a lunch with friends, and they invited someone that I had not seen for many years. I could see (and feel) this person try to discern and to "read" me. I watched her try and try again to get through my shield. I could feel the draw. I could tell that she was doing this naturally and couldn't understand why she kept hitting a brick wall. I sensed her frustration.

To break her spiritual probing, I asked her a question. She had to break her concentration in order to answer me. She naturally walks in a high level of discernment and was trying to read what I carried, not realizing that I was intentionally shielding myself from her. It was interesting to watch the scene unfold, and also fun to realize how much I had grown in my own shielding and discernment.

SHIELDING IN TIMES OF MINISTRY

Shielding is the deliberate act of protecting yourself. I gave you a couple of examples of how to do it by using your imagination for a visual shield. This is a great tool to use as a feeler. God gave us an imagination to use, and this is one way to use it. Some people have used their imagination to advance science, make music, and create beautiful art. All this for the glory of the Lord.

For counselors and those who do heart healing, this practice of shielding happens almost automatically. But as a person who walks in deliverance, I became deliberate on how I shield myself before my deliverances or any heart healing. Besides being intentional to pray for guidance, I also pray for protection over myself, the process, the person involved, and also the household (or office) where the ministry is taking place. The Lord loves heart healing, and He loves to be asked to be involved. If you find yourself in a situation where you need shielding during a deliverance or counseling session, here is a piece of advice: you do not have to beg the Lord for His protection or involvement. He is already involved, but He likes to be invited into the process.

Here is a sample protection prayer I use to shield:

Lord, Jesus Christ: I ask that a canopy of protection and your shielding be put upon me and the area that I am walking into (or currently am at). I declare that spiritual entities that are not serving the Lord Jesus Christ do not have permission to be here or observe. If there are any entities that are within this canopy but outside the human body, they are to be sent to the throne room of God for His perfect will and judgement. I ask for your angels to protect me, Lord, and I thank you in advance for your help, guidance, and revelation you will give me in this situation. Holy Spirit, please be in here and be in charge. Amen.

One of my friends, Dawn Kelly, who does heart healing Sozos, makes it a point to put on the armor of God (Ephesians 6) as a shield before she goes into places or sessions. (Sozo is a Greek word translated "saved, healed, delivered." The word is used over 100 times in the New Testament. Sozo is also the name of a ministry that aims to get to the root of things hindering your personal connection with the Father, Son, and Holy Spirit.) Dawn also always starts her sessions by ushering in the presence of God, "to dispel critters or what's in the atmosphere." The presence of the Holy Spirit is an amazing cleansing agent and a breath of fresh air. "Critters" is the term she uses to describe the demonic entities that are not invited to participate. Her prayer is like flicking bugs off your shoulders. After a session with an individual, she includes prayers of thankfulness. "Thank you, Lord, for what you did in their hearts and the truth that they have discovered. Thank you, Lord, for being in charge and I praise your holy Name."

There are also times when I have to shield myself from people that want to "draw out" my anointing or giftings. I know this sounds really weird. There is a difference between people who are curious or hungry for information about the spiritual realm and those who want the anointing or gifts without taking time to develop their own intimacy with the Lord. It reminds me of the story in Acts 8 about Simon the sorcerer who wanted to buy the gift of the Spirit by the laying on of hands. Simon was a believer, but he had no knowledge of what he was asking for. It was a heart posture, and Peter rebuked him.

I believe that people who want the anointing of leaders do not understand the journey those leaders have gone through to get to where they are. For Jesus, it is the process He is doing in our hearts that is important. Be careful not to rush into things that you are not equipped to handle. Be hungry, absolutely. But understand that we are all on a journey with the Lord. We can accelerate this process with intimacy with the Lord and by learning from other leaders. But it is the process that is most important.

DON'T TAKE ON WHAT ISN'T YOURS

I recently interviewed my friend Kristi, who is a strong feeler, about how she navigates the emotions and feelings she picks up in the atmosphere all around her. She offered some incredible wisdom.

"For me, the big thing is about identifying it (the emotion or atmosphere) and realizing that it is not mine. Once I have done that, it usually lifts. For example, I remember that I was in second year (BSSM) and I had a new neighbor move into the apartment next to me. I could tell that he was really involved in New Age and also pornography. I felt like I had been slimed and I felt the weirdness of it. Once I noticed and could identify where it was coming from, I no longer felt it or contended with it. I think I have been practicing this my whole life just to survive but did not realize it."

Kristi went on to say, "I also would shut things off. For example, I would get bad stomach aches as a child. I thought it was allergies or an illness. My family and I would go to a restaurant and as we pulled into the parking lot, my stomach problems would begin and I would say, 'No, I'm not eating here.' I didn't even want to be in the restaurant. I have often wondered if that was my feeler gift being activated, but the pieces didn't come together until I started at BSSM.

"I remember being in first year of ministry school and being overwhelmed with everything that was going on around me. But by my third year, I would walk into the first-year area and say, 'not today' and walk back out. I could feel the atmosphere and knew that I could not handle it at that time. I would make a decision based on what I could feel. I remember the teaching in first year that it is important to know what you feel before you walk into a room, that was a huge revelation to me. I was more apt to identify what I was picking up in the room instead of thinking, 'what is going on with me that I need to deal with?'"

When I asked Kristi about how she identifies where certain emotions are coming from, she shared some really interesting details. It reminded me that the way we experience the feeler gift can be different from person to person! For Kristi, she found that if she is feeling nauseous or has a spinning feeling, that may be witch-craft or a spirit of manipulation, or even New Age.

Sometimes she would have thoughts that were not her own. For example, having sexual thoughts and knowing they didn't belong to her. And of course, Kristi reiterated that understanding what belongs to us and what belongs to others comes through constant conversation with the Lord. Stay connected to Him; He will help you identify, navigate, and see patterns.

These are a few more questions that I asked Kristi, and I found her insight so powerful, I wanted to share her responses as she gave them to me:

Q: *Do you think that you need to be a born-again Christian before you can be a feeler?*
A: No, not to feel, but to understand and overcome. My jour-ney began with being born again. It's the Lord who helps us walk through the gifts He gives.

Q: *What about atmospheres? Are there atmosphere that are harder to contend with than others?*
A: My first year pastor said something so profound: "Sometimes it's not your battle, it's not your day to war. Just because you have this gift doesn't mean that every time you pick something up in the atmosphere you have to do something about it. But stay connected to the Lord and decide with Him if this is your battle." It reminded me of the example of going to the grocery store. You can have all kinds of stuff thrown at you, but it doesn't mean it's your thing. It is, however, good for you to be aware.

Sometimes I walk into an atmosphere that I identify but I have not been released from, (for example: anxiousness or fear). I go back to the Lord to see if this is mine and why He is bringing it up so that I can personally work on it. I work on it by identifying it, if I can; repent; and ask if there is anything that He is showing me. Then I can be in the clear and get out from under it. It goes back to practicing shielding. There is so much coming at you, you try to protect yourself from your own stuff. So, I learn that I don't need to deal with it. It is a protection mode. Try to stay healthy and take care of your own emotions.

> *(I found Kristi's answer here to be very confirming: one of my own revelations as a feeler is the fact that I do not need to fix everything that I become aware of. Just pay attention and learn about it with the Lord. He will tell you when it's your time to do anything).*

Q: *Do you find the feeler gift to be a hinderance or an asset?*
A: It is meant to be an asset, but it can feel like a hinderance. I can now walk in a room and gauge what is happening a lot faster with the feeler gift than if I didn't have it. If I carry something that can help or change the atmosphere, then I do. For example, I carry peace and that is easy to release. And that is such a gift.

CHAPTER EIGHT

BATTLING THE DEMONIC

Since feelers are able to pick up on negative emotions and feelings easier than most people, this gift has wreaked havoc on many feelers' lives through fear and intimidation. The demonic (or the enemy) has tried to paralyze us, keeping us stuck in a place of inaction. It is time to put on our armor of God (Ephesians 6) and take action. If you have been given this gift, then you are protected and need to proactively put on the offensive/defensive gear. You must believe in the authority that God has given you. Jesus' authority over the demonic was quite evident because He did not tolerate darkness like we do. It is time to no longer tolerate the enemy. We, as believers, are commissioned into the Kingdom of God, and like Jesus, we are given authority to defeat the kingdom of the enemy. You need to decide which kingdom you are going to operate in. And which kingdom you trust.

POWER AND AUTHORITY

Battling the enemy, the demonic, is all about understanding your authority and power. If you have accepted Jesus Christ as your Lord and Savior, then you have authority and power. It is that simple!

There are some who walk in the gifts more powerfully than others, but it all starts with the power and authority that Jesus gives us when we accept Him into our hearts. If someone you know seems to walk more powerfully, then I would deduce that it is because of the intimacy they have with the Lord. If you believe and totally trust in Him, then things happen. Your power increases. It is when the enemy sows doubt and fear into our hearts that our power may become impaired.

During the temptations of Jesus in Luke chapter 4, Satan consistently tried to sow doubt about who Jesus truly is. Christ's identity was under attack. Satan is not that inventive, but why change if it works? He is still doing that now, this time to our identities. He whispers how powerless we are, that we are not worth anything, that our prayers do not matter, and that we will not get any results when we pray. The enemy is whispering in our ears that God does not love us, that we are a bad and sinful people, that some sins are unforgivable, and so on. The enemy wants to bring in shame and feelings of condemnation.

First of all, that is all nonsense. You are powerful, and amazing, and deeply loved by God. Jesus died for your sins so that you will be free, saved, and cleansed. He paid IN FULL the price of your redemption. Every time you believe the truth about God, what He says, or find the truth within Scripture, you have defeated the enemy. It is only when we believe the lies of the enemy, that he receives power over us. Truth is a big deal.

In Job 28:12-13 it says, "But where can wisdom be found? Where does understanding dwell? No mortal comprehends its worth; it cannot be found in the land of the living." Verse 28 then says, "And he said to the human race, 'the fear of the Lord—that is wisdom, and to shun evil is understanding.'" Jesus only told the truth, and He said that He is giving us power and authority to defeat the enemy. I contend that we cannot comprehend the worth of the power and authority that we have received from Jesus. This power that God gave us is to be used to defeat the enemy so that we will be aligned with heaven. Not so that heaven aligns itself with us (like so much of mankind wishes).

We must change our mindset to grasp the full meaning and worth of what Jesus has imparted to us. I am constantly asking for more wisdom and understanding to be able to use the power and authority that Jesus gave me.

One time during a deliverance, a demon spoke audibly through the person receiving deliverance. The demon bragged about all his accomplishments over the beautiful person who was receiving prayer. He was prideful…and then he made a huge slip. He was bragging about his power and belittling mine when he said something important: "You humans don't know the power that you have." "Aha!" I thought. "Thank you very much for telling me." The demon didn't say another word after that, because he knew that I knew he had made a big mistake. The demon was trying to disempower me by bragging, but instead, I became aware and more empowered. I absolutely knew the power that I held because of the Name of Jesus Christ. By His Name, every knee must bend.

Not only did the demon confirm what I have always been told, but he solidified my own faith in God and what He has done for all human beings. When God breathed His own breath into us, He gave us part of Himself. We are made in His image.

It was not until that moment that I *fully* realized the vastness of that statement: Made in His image. Wow. To say that we believe in God, that word "believe" is an action word. Belief is not just saying the right words to placate a big God. It is confirming all that God has for us. All the love He has for us, the way He thinks about us—which is our identity, all the gifts He wants to give, all the anointing to be placed upon our shoulders, all the whispers He wants to reveal to us. He desperately wants to reveal His plans that He has for us, for you, for me.

One Scripture that I hold dear to my heart is Philippians 2:9-11: "Therefore God exalted him to the highest place and gave him the name that is above every name, that at the name of Jesus every knee should bow, in heaven and on earth and under the earth, and every tongue acknowledge that Jesus Christ is Lord, to the glory of God the Father."

That is one powerful Scripture and the mandate that we should be operating under. This is how we are to defeat the enemy. The enemy has to bend its knee to the Name of Jesus. The Name encompasses all the power, authority, and all the attributes that Jesus Christ operates in. It is His essence. He is God and He is ALL-mighty. And He has given us permission to use His Name to fight and overpower the devil. We are made in His image and have been given the signet ring of authority. We have permission to sign Jesus' Name. We have power and authority to represent the Almighty Lord. Use your power and authority wisely. You are operating in His authority, and it is a big responsibility. The more you identify with what God has already said about you and who you are, and the more you actually believe Him, the more authority you have to change things around you.

OVERCOMING LIES

Another tool we have to defeat the enemy is to take out the lies that we have partnered with. Disconnect the connection. If you have believed lies, then you have given the enemy permission to bug you. Yuck! We have all done it. Walking in the truth of God is the ultimate way of warfare. Taking out lies is a form of deliverance. It is an exchange. Exchange the lie for the truth. Take out the yuck and replace it with the good of God.

How do we expose the lies? There are a couple of ways. But be prepared to do some soul searching and exposing. Become vulnerable and not self-protecting. Some of our lies are so ingrained in us that we think they are part of our make-up and who we are. You will need to dig deep, sometimes over a period of time in order to weed them out. But God is such a gentleman. He is patient and kind and knows we are trying. He will strip things off in layers. But He loves our freedom more than our comfort.

After deliverances, I go through a two-part exercise of exposing lies that many people have swallowed. I call it the lie exercise (inventive, isn't it?). Take a piece of paper and fold it lengthwise so that it creates two columns. You can also do this in your journal. At the top of one column, write the word "Lies." (If using your journal, I recommend writing your "Lies" list on the outside column so it is easier to remove later without tearing out the entire journal page.) Remember the prayer to hear God's voice? Find it in this book and say that prayer. Then ask the Lord: "Lord, please bring to my mind the lies I am believing." Write a word or two that comes to mind and skip a line between each lie that is revealed. Write until the Lord stops speaking. Really press in to listen for these lies to be revealed.

Now, place your hand over that part of the paper that contains these lies and say a prayer of repentance. In your own words, the prayer should include the following:

1. Thank God for His answers that He gave you.
2. Repent for believing the lies that Satan and his minions have told you.
3. Repent for taking on the emotions that are associated with those lies.
4. Repent and ask forgiveness for partnering your responses or reactions to these lies.

For the second part to this exercise, write the word "Truth" at the top of the other column. For each lie that the Lord exposed, I want you to ask the Lord for HIS truth. Write His truth to every single lie that was put on the paper. Thank the Lord for His revelation.

Now, take a pair of scissors and cut the paper in half, cutting off the lie section. Rip it into shreds. They no longer exist. You are no longer walking in the reality of the lies. Every day, for the next thirty days, I want you to declare the truths you have written down over yourself, out loud. You are beginning to change your mindset of what you used to walk in. Daily declare your identity into the atmosphere. Say them out loud. Hang them on your mirror, if needed, and declare them into the heavens every day. Your new identity of truth is being formed into your mind and soul. You are transforming your mind. You have reason to celebrate!

When I originally did this exercise, I went back months later to figure out what the lies were that corresponded to the truths. Guess what? I couldn't figure out what the lies were! Miraculous healing. Then, about nine months after my deliverance, I was having a terrible time of confusion and the enemy was really doing a number on me. I finally went back to the gentleman who did my deliverance (I was still being trained by him) and talked to him about this season in my life. He said that I should do the lie exercise again. I did, and I filled up two pages worth of lies that I was believing. The reason it was two pages was not because I was walking in more lies, but because I could hear the truth more clearly from God. God was peeling the layers off that needed to be gone. God does our healing in stages, and it is a life-long procedure.

AUTHORITY IN DELIVERANCE

I want to take a moment on this topic to share a brief thought about deliverance. There are several ways of doing or partaking in deliverance, and many ministers do things differently. Regardless of how we do deliverance, and regardless of our authority and power, it is important that the participant agree to have a deliverance done in order for it to happen cleanly.

Here are a few examples of deliverance in which the participant agrees to receive ministry:

1. There is the kind of deliverance where prayers are said over you to break partnership with the demonic. There are several ministries that do this. This often results in dramatic responses like vomiting, retching, demonic voices, etc. I do not do this kind of deliverance. My deliverances include prayers but are peaceful and orderly. But I have seen anointed ministers do this kind of deliverance.

2. Every time you exchange a lie for the truth, that is a type of deliverance. The definition of

deliverance is, "the action of being rescued or set free."[4]

3. The expression of "love the hell right out of them" is so true! This is a deliverance. To show the love of Christ and have it imbedded into the hearts of those you are loving can be healing and imperative. It is amazing what transformation takes place when we realize how powerful and healing the love of Jesus can be.

4. The act of forgiveness is a deliverance. You are letting go of unforgiveness that can have a hold on you. The enemy can use unforgiveness to embitter your heart and then he has access to you. By forgiving, you are cutting off that access. Sozo is an inner healing ministry that is excellent with this kind of deliverance. The Sozo minister will walk you through offenses and unforgiveness toward others, your own emotions, and even yourself. It is a wonderful way of revealing soul hurts and traumas.

5. One last kind of deliverance can be so quick and easy: tell the demon to go in the Name of Jesus and pour blessings back on the person being ministered to. This can be a temporary solution, depending upon their understanding of being free and keeping up this freedom. The demons will come knocking at their door again just to see if they will crack it open to look to see who is knocking.

4   https://languages.oup.com/google-dictionary-en/

Whole books have been written about each one of these points. But it mostly comes down to this: Our freedom is dependent upon intimacy with the Lord. As we lean into the Lord and believe in Him, giving our yes and surrendering, then the Lord can heal our souls and hearts. It requires an agreement to walk out the process of healing, a willingness to be vulnerable, and allowing God to fill up our faith tank. I encourage you to go after deliverance for yourself, and not just for those you feel you should minister to. Deliverance gives you a jump start on your own growth and stops the voices in your head. Choose to believe what God says about you and stop the inner monologue that goes on in your mind.

MAKE A CONFESSION OF FAITH WITH YOUR MOUTH

To affect the strategies of the enemy, you must speak out loud your prayers or declarations. This is why I had you declare the prayers at the beginning of this book out loud. When you talk to God, you *can* do it within your mind (because He KNOWS everything), but any time you want to direct anything towards the enemy or make a declaration of faith, you need to speak (or whisper) orally. The devil cannot read your mind. But he does know you.

For example, when you look at your spouse during a situation, you often can read their mind and know what they are thinking. Either because you know them so well, or by their expressions or body language. While the enemy cannot read your mind, he has the same ability to read your reactions and body language. He has been around you since you were very small. He has seen your body language and how you think. Therefore, any defeating or warfare you are doing concerning the enemy, it must be done out loud. Your voice affects the spiritual realm around you. It is a powerful force and should be unleashed against the enemy. Do not discount the value of your voice!

There have been many times during prayer ministry after a service that I have picked off the enemy before I pray for an individual. Does the participant know this? No, because I whisper this part of my prayer. I will let the individual know that I will pray quietly for a moment, so as to not alarm them. They do not need to know what I am feeling and what engagement I am doing to combat the enemy. Once I have prayed quietly about what needs to be "taken off," I then begin to pray openly so that the individual can partner with the prayer that I am "putting back on." What we "put back on" will always be the truth of what the Lord says about them. It is always loving and kind as I pray for what their needs are.

In Romans 10:9-10, Paul talks about the profession of faith. "If you declare with your mouth, 'Jesus is Lord,' and believe in your heart that God raised him from the dead, you will be saved. For it is with your heart that you believe and are justified, and it is with your mouth that you profess your faith and are saved."

This is why our confession of faith needs to be done with our mouths, out loud, to be able to affect and break the agreement of the enemy. By speaking out loud, we are breaking a contract that was made with the enemy. The contract that was made with Adam. We are intentionally breaking one contract and making a new contract with the Lord Jesus Christ, and this must be done orally.

Confess with your mouth. Almost everything that comes out of your mouth is either a blessing or a curse. Be careful with your words. Make sure that everything that comes out of your mouth is a blessing and, if by chance you accidently say something that is not nice (a curse), you can reverse it quickly. "Lord, I didn't mean what I just said. Forgive me. I ask to take that back and I want to bless (that person or that situation, etc)."

EXPOSE THE DEMONIC

One of the main weapons of the enemy is fear. Fear causes us to feel immobilized or the need to be hidden. The sense of panic and fear that many feelers have lived with is asphyxiating, especially as a child. It seems to take your breath away and it becomes suffocating. Many times, as adults, we can reason our way out of these feelings and understand that logically there is nothing to be fearful about. But it is a battle of the mind.

For many of us, we have been shingled with a sign that says, "anxiety," but, in actuality, the anxiety we feel or express may be a byproduct of the atmosphere that we are standing in. Many children are learning this new kind of labeling language, from either a parent, teachers, or their peers. No one has considered the spiritual atmosphere that the child is contending or accidentally partnering with. I understand that anxiety and depression have a physical diagnosis and there are mitigating factors to contend with, but I also feel that anxiety and depression are symptoms of the demonic atmosphere that is being administered. People who struggle with anxiety and depression may be incapable of navigating the atmosphere that they are feeling, or they do not know the tools to use to protect themselves.

Calling out the demonic and its strategies is one way to defeat it. Dawna DeSilva would say in her lectures, "I see you and I will not partner with you." In other words, Dawna would feel the atmosphere and expose it. The demonic loves to hide, and by calling it out, you expose it. Call on the mighty Name of the Lord Jesus Christ.

Bring the light of the Kingdom into the situation. Take out and put back in. When Jesus released the Spirit, He pushed out the darkness. Whatever you are experiencing, pray for the opposite. Depression? Pray for comfort, lightness, and joy. "I see you, depression and sadness. Go, in the Name of Jesus. I pray joy over my life and a changing of my attitude." Put on worship music, take a walk, literally talk to Jesus about this. My friend Jenna once shared on a podcast, "Invite Jesus into your darkness and believe that He will take your hand and walk you out of it. Be thankful and be prepared for the process. Get unstuck with praise, faith, and thanksgiving to Him. His love changes everything." This is so true.

In exposing the demonic, however, it is important that we not act like there is a demon behind every bush. My dear friend, Dawn Kelly, said it best: "Don't look for the darkness but instead be attentive to the Light. Switch your thinking. Of course, you will feel the enemy, and as you do, switch your mindset on Jesus, who is the best role model of atmosphere changing. Jesus always looked up to the Father instead of tolerating the enemy on the ground. When you look towards the Father, the atmosphere shifts. It is the exposure to light."

One way to switch your mindset when dealing with the demonic is to ask the Lord, "God what are you doing?" This allows us to see and call out the demonic, but partner with what God is doing instead of focusing on what the enemy is doing. Turn your eyes to the Lord. There are times when I literally look upwards so that my physical body makes the shift into the spiritual realm.

When I was learning to ride my horse, my trainer would often say to turn my head the way I wanted my horse to go. I wouldn't need to turn my body or use my reins but just turn my head and my horse would sense my directive. This is also true in the spiritual.

Turn your head or your eyes upwards. You are signaling that you are turning your mind, soul, and spirit towards the Lord.

I was listening to the radio recently and there was a little devotional moment on the radio show. One of the things the host said was that whatever you feed, it manifests and grows. And whatever you starve, it will shrink. This is especially applicable to the feeler gift and the demonic. If you are constantly "feeding" the enemy with fears and the anxiety that he is putting on you, you will multiply and make it grow. You are "feeding" the enemy power over you.

We can recognize and call out the demonic, but the more we give into it with fear and anxiety, it gives the demonic a thrill. Yet, we do not want to ignore the enemy as though he does not exist. It is a paradox. You must find the fine line to walk—acknowledge the enemy, recognize him, but do not partner with him. The demonic that you feel is there for your information. Ask God what you should do with that information.

One way to change the direction of this info is the way you acknowledge God in the situation. Just like you acknowledged the enemy, recognized him, and did not partner with him, the opposite is true for God. Acknowledge God by calling out one of His many names, recognizing that He is involved because you have turned your eyes towards Him, and absolutely *do* partner with Him by asking Him questions.

The same truth applies to the feeler gift. You want it to grow and be useful to you. Acknowledge the feeler gift and the emotions you feel and know that they are there to learn from. You do not need to "wear" the feelings/emotions but use them for what they are good for: information and a way to connect with and learn from God. The feeler gift is a tool to use and grow in.

GOD IS YOUR COVERING

One of my dear friends, Jill Lewis, wrote down a vision that God gave her.

"I was sitting in church as I do most Sundays. My mom was on my right and my husband on my left. The pressure of the room was felt from all sides as we sang from the hymnal. I had my eyes closed, asking God, 'What is it You are doing in the room?'

"Suddenly, I was sitting next to Jesus. He had His arm around me, and we were the only ones in the room. It was pitch black as we gazed into the starry sky. As we gazed up at the sky, I saw what I thought to be a shooting star. Then Jesus pointed it out excitedly, 'Here comes one!' As the point of movement got closer, I realized it was a demon and it was headed straight for us. Just as it was about to land, it hit an invisible dome, bounced off and tumbled away squealing into the darkness. Then Jesus burst out laughing and I joined Him.

"This scene was repeated several times and I became more and more aware of the protection around me. The demonic could not get to me and the best thing I could do is hang out with Jesus and laugh. As we continued to watch, another demon hit the dome hard, and instead of bouncing off as the others had, he smashed against the dome like a bug on a windshield, groaning as he slid down the side. It was obvious I was loved and protected.

"A short time later Covid-19 hit, and I was an essential worker. I was challenged as I went to work each day because the fear in the air was thick and hard to maneuver through. In my time of devotion with the Lord, He took me back to that vision. He reminded me of my covering and protection. I'm covered, I'm protected. I have a choice now. I can choose to partner with fear, or I can choose to believe what God is telling me and walk in that confidence and protection."

I love Jill's description of her encounter with God. Jill is an immense feeler and she had to learn from God about this gift. Let me tell you, we have had many discussions about the gift He "dumped" on her. She was not happy about it and had a lot of difficulty with it. But now, she has such intimacy with the Lord, and she uses this tremendous gift in her ministry. I am quite inspired by her familiarity with Him. With each one of us, He encounters us differently and gives us what we need at that time.

As we learn how to step into our feeler gift and authority in battling the enemy, it is so important to remember that God is our covering. Just as Jill's vision demonstrates, we can choose to partner with fear over what we see and feel, or we can believe God when He tells us we are protected, we have authority, and we can use our gift with confidence.

CHAPTER NINE

TAKING BACK TERRITORY

We talked about intercession as one of the main reasons you have a feeler gift. I'm going to take you into a new level and layer of your intercession. I want to talk to you about taking back territory, in the spiritual and the physical. God revealed this truth through situations that I had with Him. It was a process over several years, but the revelation is outstanding.

A couple of years after my visit to the Oregon Country Fair, I began attending the Bethel School of Supernatural Ministry. Each year, the students are given a service assignment where they serve in various capacities in the local community or with nearby non-profits. For my first-year ministry service, I was assigned to Reno, Nevada. Our group would drive over once a month for the weekend to help in an organization that prevented sex trafficking and helped women who have been trafficked. We would do street evangelism and help out in any capacity that the ministry needed.

Later in the year, we had the opportunity to help in the Spring-time New Age Fair in Reno. I was a little nervous about this, especially after going to the Oregon Country Fair. It is one thing to walk and pray but it is another thing to engage in talking to New Age people, spiritualists, and those involved in the occult. There was a Christian man who had a booth at the fair, and he would minister in a covert way. After working at that fair, I realized that it is possible to minister to "those" people quite easily; I just needed to be solidly armored up.

In fact, ministering to people involved in New Age and the occult is not much different than ministering and evangelizing to people on the streets. It requires us to use different language and not "Christian-ese." I found that people are thirsty for the God of the Universe just as much as we are, but in their search, they went down a different path. It was fun to show them how much our God loves them and how amazing His power is, and to see their faces light up when Jesus healed or touched their hearts brought us such joy and satisfaction. A few years later, I was able to lead students on ministry trips to work at the booth. Amazing things would happen: healings, prophetic words, dream interpretations, deliverance, and even a few salvations. The students would learn and grow so much spiritually and in their gifts.

Part of using our feeler gift in this setting is understanding the territory and atmospheres around us. Sometimes this means learning to feel the atmosphere that others bring as we minister to them, and other times it means learning to feel the territorial atmosphere of a place. This is possible as we open ourselves up to our feeler gift. I have visited spiritually depressed areas that were tragically hurt during WW-II, and I could feel the territorial evil that was done to the land. Just like we can feel territorial evil spirits, we can also feel the angelic or what the Holy Spirit has injected into a territory.

I went to England in 2019 and had the opportunity to drive over to Wales to visit Moriah Chapel. This is the chapel where the Welsh Revival was led by Evan Roberts in 1904 to 1905. My friend

Kristi McCracken and I had a private tour from a lady who had lived her whole life in this small town and still played the piano for the church services. When I entered the property, I "felt" the holiness of the Lord upon that place. It was solemn, and heavy with the oil of prayers and worship. We both could feel the angelic presence that was there because of all that had happened in the past. There was an intensity in the atmosphere of all that was deposited through prayer and supplication.

We did not want to "disturb" the presence that was there inside the chapel. We intentionally engaged in what the spiritual atmosphere was showing us. We had another ministry school alumni that drove us there, who is not necessarily a big feeler, and he did not experience the magnitude of what we were feeling. He is more of an intellectual and he experienced the chapel through that lens. But his takeaway was the same as ours: we were standing in a holy place. He could sense it even if he could not feel it as Kristi and I did.

PRAYING OVER THE LAND

After completing my second year at BSSM, the Lord impressed upon me to go back to the Oregon Country Fair to "pray over the land" in a specific way. I had been back to the fair with my family the past few years and the atmosphere didn't bother me as much. This was also not my first time praying over land. The Lord would often direct me to walk and pray over certain areas of Redding, or other cities I visited. Of course, my yes was to the Lord and my good friend, Sheryl, consented to go with me to Eugene, Oregon. It was a five-hour drive, one way, and we decided to do this in one day. We realized that it was going to be a ten-hour road trip broken up by several hours walking around the fair. Yikes!

Several peculiar things happened as we drove north on the

freeway that solidified the fact we were on the right mission. As we drove up Interstate 5, a crow flew into my windshield. Sheryl and I just looked at each other and began to laugh. For other people, I think it would have freaked them out, but we knew the enemy's tactics and knew he wouldn't be successful. When we got to the fair, we had to get our tickets at the will call booth. As we were standing in line, we had just taken a step forward when a big gust of wind came and blew a large, heavy sign down that was next to us, hitting a young boy on the head. Right away we started talking to the parents and the boy was crying. We were concerned about his injuries. Sheryl said to them, "Do you want me to pray over your son?" I remember the parents looking at us as though we were aliens. Oops, wrong venue. Sheryl and I knew that the sign was meant to fall on us.

Once we entered the fairgrounds, Sheryl felt the atmosphere intensely. She turned to me and told me that she would need to listen to worship music for a while. She put on her earbuds as I went to watch the cloggers do their dance moves (and to pray). I totally understood where she was coming from, and I was surprised at the fact that I had already shielded myself from the atmosphere and it did not bother me. I knew the Lord had directed me there and I was fully protected.

After a bit, Sheryl joined me, and we began to walk the fair and pray over the land and the atmosphere. We noticed two dragonflies that kept chasing and flying around us. We looked up the prophetic meaning of the dragonfly and it means transformation or change. We began to declare transformation over the fair and welcoming in the Kingdom of God. Once we did this, the dragonflies flew away. We got a kick out of that!

At one point, Sheryl felt the Lord tell her to look for a yellow sign. We found a sign about half an hour later at the intersection of a path. We looked around and there was a rock ledge we could sit on and pray. Directly in front of us was a booth full of witchcraft and warlock paraphernalia. They had clothing, symbols, and jewelry. Sheryl and I looked at each other in amazement. It was a wonder how God directed us there! I started praying that anyone that came into their booth would walk out and not buy anything. I watched as people would come in, and then walk out. It was becoming entertaining to watch how God was working.

I also prayed for a woman sitting in the booth who I could tell had authority as a witch. She would sit in her chair as though it was a throne and people would come into the booth and pay her homage. As we prayed, I watched her keep looking around as though she "felt" my prayers. I could tell that she was agitated. At one stage, she got up to go in the back of the booth and grab marijuana to smoke. I nudged Sheryl and said, "Look, she needs to medicate herself." Eventually, she got up and left the booth.

Meanwhile, Sheryl was praying for the man running the booth and selling the products. He was quite disturbed that no one was buying anything. He left for about ten minutes and then returned, anxious. After a while, he tried to prompt buyers into the booth. We watched him become more and more agitated. After about an hour of praying, we felt that we were done. Not once did anyone see us sitting on the rock wall only a few feet away. No one turned their gaze towards us; it was as though we were hidden.

Two Scriptures came to mind as we prayed. The first was Psalm 17:8, "Keep me as the apple of your eye; hide me in the shadow of your wings." The second was Isaiah 51:16, "I have put my words in your mouth and covered you with the shadow of my hand—I who set the heavens in place, who laid the foundations of the earth, and who say to Zion, 'You are my people.'" We felt that we had accomplished something that day, even though we had no idea what it was.

The next year, I returned to the Oregon Country Fair to continue my prayer walk. The Lord was beginning to plant the seed to bring a ministry group there in the future to prophesy and heal. I knew that I needed to get the atmosphere ready; "to take back the land." As I walked and prayed, I went looking for the witchcraft booth. It was gone! It had been in a prime location of the fair and had obviously been located there for many years. I marveled at how the Lord works and I praised His Holy Name. He knew that I needed to see this for myself; the evidence of what intercession prayer can do.

The next year, I did not return to the fair due to obligations and international travel, but I assembled a small team to go with me the following year. There were six of us that fanned out among the throngs of people to heal, to prophesy, and whatever the Holy Spirit led us to do, which naturally opened the door for us to talk about God. It was exciting to hear the testimonies. As we planned for the next year, COVID-19 hit our nation and everything shut down, including the fair. The fair is currently having problems due to the land use laws and their status is unsure. Who knows what the future will hold?

REDEEMING TERRITORIES

God needs us to pray and take back territory that has been dedicated to the enemy. As feelers, it is our job to sense these territories, and pray to take back the territory where evil has taken place. Repent for the evil that was conducted on that land and ask God what needs to be brought back into the land to bless it. When we talk about "taking back territory" or praying over the land, I am not only talking about the physical ground, but I am talking about the spiritual atmosphere that is around the area.

My friend Jenna Winston, who has the gifting of a seer, does this very naturally and she shared an incredible testimony of territorial prayer and redemption. It was New Year's Day 2015, and Jenna was in her first year of BSSM. When her roommate returned home at 2:00 a.m., Jenna awoke suddenly with three angels standing over her. Before she even took off her eye cover, she knew they were there. She took off her eye cover and one of the angels said to her, "You are going to Reno to put a dollar in a slot machine."

Jenna was surprised. Her first thought was, "Oh yah, because God is going to have me go to Sin City and gamble on New Year's." And then the angel said, "Oh, there's that religious spirit." Jenna then saw a picture of a slot machine in her mind. Even though she had never been to Reno, she knew that was the slot machine she was supposed to go to.

Redding, California to Reno, Nevada is a three-and-a-half-hour drive. Jenna didn't have a car, so she knew the only way to get there would be with her roommate, Holly, who had just gone to bed and often slept in late. Jenna didn't want to wake her with this sudden mission. However, at about 7:00 or 7:30 in the morning, her roommate sat up and said, "We are going to go on a journey, aren't we?" Her spirit already knew. Jenna told her about the angels, and Holly said, "Let's go!"

They set off, inviting their other housemate, Val, along for the adventure. As they drove to Reno, many different kinds of angels came along with them, as if they were joining the journey. When they got to Reno, the angels led them to the exact slot machine in the right hotel that the angel previously showed them. In her mind, Jenna thought that something big would happen—like she would win millions of dollars and feed the world and save everybody. She put the dollar in the machine, and nothing happened. No money came out of the machine. It was so anti-climactic after the drive and the big build up with all the angels. It felt like the biggest let down ever!

They were tired, hungry, and disappointed as they left the hotel. As they drove away, Holly accidentally turned down a one-way street in the wrong direction, but as she did, Jenna felt like someone had punched her in the gut. She knew God was speaking something important to her. She looked out the window and saw a territorial stronghold with her naked eye. She had previously seen such things from a distance, but this was up close, spread out over half of a ballpark and a huge baseball statue outside the park. The territorial stronghold looked like a melted Jabba the Hut. It was the weirdest thing ever. It had so much demonic and spiritual around it and mixed with it.

In that moment, Jenna knew exactly what they were supposed to do. They parked the car and got out, standing on the sidewalk facing the stronghold. As Jenna turned and looked up, she saw an army of angels on top of all the Reno buildings and parking garages and everything within her sight. Every angel held arrows and quivers. That was the first time she fully understood the Scripture, "For he will command his angels concerning you to guard you in all your ways" (Psalm 91) and she realized that they were all waiting for her to give the "go ahead."

She was so stunned that she tried to describe to her roommates what she was seeing and feeling. Together, they decided to pretend that they had bows and arrows as well. They positioned their bows and said "One, two, three," and shot their spiritual arrows—along with the angels—at the territorial stronghold. It was the most beautiful thing Jenna had ever seen. As the stronghold began to break up, demons were loosed from it, and many of the angels began to fight with them. Jenna was literally watching a spiritual battle unfold in front of her, like a battle scene from a movie or as we would envision battles that took place in the Bible. It was unbelievable. She and her roommates stood weeping as she described the present-day Bible story unfolding in front of them.

Afterward, they got back in the car, exhausted but satisfied, when suddenly the first three angels that she saw in her bedroom appeared and told Jenna she should go to Lake Tahoe. "What?!" she thought. She told her roommates and they all agreed to the next step in the journey which is approximately forty-five minutes away from Reno.

This time as they drove, angels kept appearing and saying the words "snow globe" repeatedly. They weren't sure what it meant or what they should be looking for in Tahoe. When they pulled into town, Jenna saw a stronghold on a hotel similar to the one she had seen in Reno. Thinking that was their destination, she started to direct Holly toward the hotel, but the angels said again, "Snow globe!"

Tired and grumpy, the girls weren't sure what to do. Finally, Holly said, "I'm just going to Google 'Reno and Tahoe and snow globe' and see what comes up." Jenna snapped at her and said, "Oh yah, Holly, because angels use Google."

Sure enough, she typed her search into Google and discovered that there is a Snow Globe festival that happens every year, on the twenty-ninth, thirtieth, and thirty-first of December. As it was January first, they were thinking that they missed it, but the angels continued to insist that they go there.

They found out where the festival was held and drove through the snow and ice to the campground. The venue opened up onto a huge field that looked like the aftermath of a snowy Woodstock.

The place was huge, as though it was a massive city, and Jenna felt a darkness looming over the field and city. It was as far as her eyes could see. She felt intense emotions of death and destruction, greed and power.

She wanted her roommates, and not just her—the seer—to experience what she was seeing. Knowing that they are feelers, she began to instruct them, "With your closed eyes and using your spiritual eyes, what do you guys see?" Both girls began to describe what they felt. It was exactly what Jenna was seeing.

"I'm going to get out and I'm going to pray," said Val, getting out of the car and walking around. Holly seemed very alert, so Jenna asked her was she was feeling. "It feels like my prayers are stopped. It feels like sadness and desperation."

A few minutes later, Val returned to the car and said, "It feels so weird, but as I walk, I feel like I'm fine and then I stop, and it feels like my prayers are stopped." They both described the same exact thing that was happening.

Jenna thought perhaps there was going to be another army of angels with bows and quivers of arrows, but no. Instead, the Lord said, "No, you need to know how powerful you are." Instead of coming against the demonic, binding and casting and breaking down, they started to worship and pray in tongues. They were releasing a heart of worship more than praying against the principalities and strongholds. Together, the girls began to connect to the Father's heart through worship.

With her eyes closed, and in her mind, Jenna pictured their voices piercing the darkness with white lights, breaking it apart. As she felt the darkness begin to break, she opened her eyes and saw a dark cloud that faded into clear. Instead of breaking into pieces, the darkness became lighter and lighter, until it disappeared and was gone. At the same time, Val and Holly watched with their natural eyes as the moonlight became brighter and brighter, even more than was normal. What a confirmation.

We don't always know the long-term effects of these moments when the Lord calls us to pray over a territory and redeem it for His glory. However, two years later, I was with Jenna on New Year's Day. We happened to be passing through Las Vegas from Phoenix, and we stopped at Mandalay Bay for some food. We were in a long buffet line that snaked back and forth, when we found ourselves next to a group of guys laughing and talking. Jenna and I were chatting when suddenly her ear caught the men's conversation.

They were saying, "Man, I thought you always went to the Snow Globe thing every year." Another guy said, "Yeah, but last year it was lame and cheesy. It used to be that we would get seven to eight people stacked in a shower, all puking on each other and loving it and getting rocked out of our minds, but last year it was so boring."

We were absolutely rocked. We knew that God lined it up for Jenna to hear that conversation, right in that moment. It was as though the Lord was saying, "Look what happened!" That was such a gift. Jenna called Holly on FaceTime, and she was just as shocked. We found out later that Snow Globe was never the same after that.

Since my experience at the Oregon Country Fair, Moriah Chapel, and hearing Jenna's story about Snow Globe, I have taken many domestic and international trips and I pray over the land wherever my feet stand. I may not "see" what happens as the result of my prayers, but I know without a shadow of a doubt that things do change. I have taken trips to Warsaw, Poland and to Prague, Czech Republic to pray over the city and the remnants of concentration camps. I have traveled around Europe also. I know that anywhere that I set my feet on the land, I have the authority to change the atmosphere. I repent on behalf of any evil done to the land and pray blessings and declarations.

CHAPTER TEN

THERE IS
ALWAYS MORE

I recently took a team of students with me on a ministry trip to southern Washington. It was interesting to activate my students in their feeler gift. One student said "I don't think I'm a feeler. I don't really feel anything." I asked him if he had feelings of love. As he processed that, I could feel the pieces of the puzzle land in place in his mind and spirit! He began to lean into his feeler gift and ask questions.

In order to help them continually hone their understanding of the feeler gift, I would also ask the students what they felt as we drove into different cities. We stayed overnight in Vancouver, Washington, but crossed over the river into Portland, Oregon to minister and I asked about the atmosphere. Many of them felt the heaviness and the territorial spirit that was over the region. This one small activity had awoken their new senses of the feeler gift and they were rewarded with confirmations.

Growing in this gift requires both connection with God and community. You need your "tribe" to talk about these encounters and also to challenge each other on how we pray or interact with the Lord. I have a group of friends that I get together with often and talk about what the Lord is doing in each one of our lives. I learn so much from my dear friends because God is not a cookie cutter God. He is both different and the same with people. We cannot put a limit on His actions.

The "tribe" that you get together with must be in the same type of culture that you are in. For example: I would not get together with new age people or spiritualists and process about the intimate things that God is doing in my life. I have nothing against these friends (and I have friends that are in that realm), but they are not from the same culture that I am currently involved with. I am not prejudiced, I am careful. Especially when I am processing things that the Lord is doing. I want to connect with individuals I can learn from. I am in constant amazement at how the Lord works or what He says to each person. You need to find your tribe to learn and discover the multi-layer kind of God He is.

Some may ask: what happens if I cannot find my tribe or community of like-minded believers? And I will say that they are out there, ready to be discovered. But it does take effort and expanding your borders. There are people that are in the same boat as you, but unless you ask questions of your friends or other believers, how else will you find them? Organize a study group with this book and invite others to go through it with you. You may need to visit other churches or sign up for conferences to learn and interact with other attendees. If you have a willingness to learn, God will make a way. There is always more to learn and discover about your gift!

CHILDREN AND THE FEELER GIFT

For those of you who are realizing that you have carried this gift for many years, you may be remembering moments from childhood when your feeler gift was misunderstood. Or, for those of you with children, perhaps you are recognizing this gift in your own child! Children are incredibly gifted and have had a hard time navigating and learning about their gifts, especially when parents do not believe in the Holy Spirit, the gifts of the Spirit, or do not understand what is going on in the spiritual realm.

If I would have known what I know now when my children were young, I would have parented much differently. Even the knowledge of the Holy Spirit giving gifts would have changed the way I raised my children. There is no junior Holy Spirit. Kids get the full measurement of the Spirit when He comes upon them. And children are born with gifts. My own opinion is that most babies have the seer gift. If you ever watch a child observe a room or other people, it can be quite revealing. They will begin to watch the angelic in the room.

When I take my grandkids to a restaurant, I watch them as they look at people coming into the restaurant or walking near them. I watch them pull back or lean forward, be interested in the person, or want to look away. I notice the relaxed expressions on their faces, or sometimes a look of fear. I have paid attention to them noticing the atmospheric changes that happen around them. During church services, I watch as they are drawing or playing and then suddenly the atmosphere changes and they look up and around to figure out what it was that changed. Kids are a great resource because they do not filter. As adults, we can learn a lot just by observing their behavior.

However, it is important to note that things begin to change around the ages of four to six. Kids either turn off the gifts or hide them. We need to be vigilant to nurture the gifts and keep them growing. But if they turn it off, no worries. We certainly do not want to pressure a child to keep a gift going if they don't want it. God holds their gifts until He is ready for them to be used. The off switch happens usually about the time the child goes to school. Whether it is from peer pressure, school discouragement, or society in general, that is when I have most noticed a child shut their gifts down. As adults, we have the privilege of helping walk our children through this season, teaching them about the beauty of the gifts God has given them.

We also have an opportunity to take back territory in our gifts that may have been stolen from us as children. I mentioned earlier that the gift of the feeler is multidimensional because there are so many facets to the feeler gift. With a seer gift, for example, you experience different levels of understanding based on what you see. A feeler, however, has an enormous amount of information to sift through and be entrusted with. You may feel or have a sense of "knowing" that something is happening, and that you need to access. Please do not become overwhelmed with this directional information, because the more you learn, the easier it becomes. You will develop "muscle memory" and begin to do and think automatically. That takes a bit of time, but just think how many years the enemy has had this gift under control. Well, no more! We are going to take back territory.

One of the ways you are gaining territory is by reading this book. The more knowledge you gain and understand, the more you receive the territory back that you gave away. You did not mean to give it away, but the enemy is greedy. You gave away territory when you gave up and allowed the enemy to assault you. You believed the lies that you were an emotional child, etc. If that rings true, know that you are already winning back the gift that God has given you!

HOW THE GIFTS ARE INTERTWINED

When I was learning about the gift of prophecy and began to operate in it, I would interweave the gift of knowledge throughout my prophetic words I was giving. I thought I was only giving a prophecy. It wasn't until someone pointed out what I was doing that I realized that I was operating in the gift of the word of knowledge. In fact, I didn't know about the word of knowledge at that time. It was one of those slap-on-the-forehead kinds of moments.

The gifts of the Spirit are intertwined. There will be times that your feeler gift will activate you into a prophetic word. Or perhaps you'll get a word of knowledge, but God will elaborate on it using your feeler gift. They all work together so beautifully as the Lord seeks to encounter us and those around us.

Prophecy, like the feeler gift, is one of the discernment gifts. For your prophetic gift, you must be listening to God, but also discerning whether you are to release a word that you are hearing now or hold onto it. Just like you must navigate whether your feelings are meant for intercession or action. Kind of like fishing—hold the word (or feelings) in your basket or catch and release it to a person.

Understanding how the gifts are intertwined will make things easy to know what you need to pray when you are ministering to others. When you are a feeler on the prayer ministry line in church, for example, you only need to close your eyes and feel what is happening with the person in front of you. What you need to pray is usually the opposite of what you're feeling. Many think this is a form of the "word of knowledge" mentioned in 1 Corinthians 12, but you are discerning and using your feeler gift.

The word of knowledge is also a gift from the Holy Spirit, and it is information or revelation that you receive from Him that you would not have otherwise known concerning a person or situation. You literally partner with the Holy Spirit to receive a word of knowledge. The word of knowledge is a high-level gift that the Holy Spirit gives because you must solely rely on His revelation. You must have a personal and intimate connection with the Lord to get these revelations, since they come from Him. This is only my personal opinion, but I believe that the word of knowledge gift is given later in your life and not given to you at birth. Whereas other gifts from the Holy Spirit can be given at birth, but not always. The gift of prophecy can be interwoven with the gift of knowledge, but not always. What is important is understanding that God will use you however He sees fit and being open to how the gifts work together is key!

I will not go into prophecy or the other gifts since there are several great books you can read about these gifts. I highly recommend any of Kris Vallotton's books. One of my favorites is *The Supernatural Ways of Royalty*. It talks about your own identity in Christ. I had no idea about the old thoughts (and lies) that had been planted inside of me, and this book transformed me. A couple of Kris's other books that would be good to read are, *Fashioned to Reign* and *Heavy Rain*. Any of Kris's prophetic manuals are very helpful.

Another good resource is Dan McCollam and the Prophetic Company. Dano is a fascinating and talented man formerly from Vacaville, California. He has recently moved to Texas. He is a pastor, prophet, and a worship leader. God has gifted him with the talent to be able to pick up any instrument and know how to play it. He is highly intelligent and has studied the supernatural within the physical realm.

And of course, I must call out Graham Cooke for his amazing prophetic gift and the books he writes are beyond great. Graham has several sermon series, but be prepared to stop the audio several times to write a note or just ponder what he says because he will blow your mind. Graham is similar to Bill Johnson from Bethel Church; they both have this way of making "drop the mic" statements that make your jaw drop and at the same time make your gray matter expand. I am immensely thankful that I have been exposed to these amazing and humble leaders. Bill Johnson has the gift of revelation. He is the humblest and most giving man I have ever experienced. He thrives on community. Any of Bill's books are must-read and very revealing. Your growth will be immense.

Finally, if you want to learn more about declarations and the power of the declared word, the master of declarations are Steve and Wendy Backlund. They are a phenomenal husband and wife team that will empower you to make declarations in the atmosphere, upon your life, and your identity. Steve has a unique anointing to release hope and joy. The Backlund's material will provide a great backdrop to understanding your authority in shifting atmospheres through declarations.

INTENTIONALITY OF INTIMACY

Throughout this book, I have talked quite a bit about intimacy with the Lord. For some, this is an unknown concept to grasp. For others, it is like second nature, and they cannot understand why anyone wouldn't want to connect to the Lord. And still for others, they know the God of the Bible, but they also know there is more about Him to learn. They truly want to *know* Him.

In my first year of BSSM, pastor Kris Vallotton talked about intimacy. He said that intimacy is "into me you see." That is a great way to describe intimacy: to know someone enough that they can really see into your core person at a level of closeness. This is the level of relationship and intimacy we should seek to have with the Lord.

I can honestly say that I am intentional to have my time with the Lord every morning. I sit in my bedroom and take out my Bible and my journal. I get a Bible verse, write it in my journal, and then begin to break it apart and chew on it. I put my prayer requests in the journal, my thoughts, my questions, and hopefully, His answers. My journaling becomes my love letter to the Lord. I have done this for years and years. I do experience dry spells, at times; moments when I feel there is a disconnect, and I try to figure out why. These do not last very long because I am intentional in my pursuit of intimacy with God.

Today, as I write this, I was in a stalemate kind of state, and the Lord told me to change things up. I looked up my scripture and drove to a park where I could take a walk. I put on the audio reading of that scripture and listened to it. I felt a vibrance in my prayer of His love for me. I turned my heart to Him, and He gave me strategies of how to pray and worship Him. I prayed forgiveness over my country, and I prayed for my leaders. I asked God to bless them. I prayed over the persecution of Christians in other countries. And before I knew it, an hour had passed by.

Then the Lord began to talk to me about remembrance. As He did, I began to see a new way to clarify intimacy with the Lord, and how to share it with those of you who may be struggling to understand how to develop this intimacy.

Let's start with a quick activation:

Think of an old or current boyfriend/girlfriend, or your spouse. I want you to turn your mind to when you first began to date this person, when you

*realized that you really liked them. Remember how
you couldn't get them out of your mind. Remember
how the very thought of this person would bring a
smile to your face or a flutter in your stomach. Your
mind would shift and think of this person several
times during the day, even if it was only for a few
seconds. When you were newly in love, your mind
would constantly drift towards that person. Try to
remember those moments.*

When the Lord was at the last supper with his best friends,
He talked about the bread and the wine and to partake of it in
remembrance of Him. As Christians, we do this with communion.
We partake of communion in remembrance of Him. We shift our
minds to remember and focus on what He has done for us. It is a
mind shift, not only to His sacrifice (this is what communion is all
about) and the high price that He paid for us, but also to memories
of how much He loves us. Just like you can recall those early days
of intimacy with your spouse or significant other and how often
your mind thought (or still does think) of them throughout the
day, Jesus wants you to shift your mind to Him, and take up your
daily bread with Him!

Intimacy is shifting our minds towards God. Even if it is only for
a moment during your busy workday. Let Him bring a smile to your
face. Be aware of the emotions attached to this momentary shift. Let
it bring fulfillment, love, blessings, companionship, a friendship, joy,
a funny thought that He brings to your mind.

I remember how one of my pastors in BSSM would set alarms
on his phone several times during the day. I think he did it every
few hours or at strategic times; his alarm would go off on his phone.

And was with him enough times to know that these alarms would go off often. Every time the alarm went off, he would redirect his mind and shift it to acknowledging the Lord. He did not stop everything that he was doing, or stop in mid-conversation and say, "Hold on, I have to pray." But that alarm was his reminder to focus on God, and there was a shift in the atmosphere that happened during that time.

Sometimes, he would simply whisper the Lord's name and then go on with whatever he was doing. It was the act of reaching out to turn off his alarm that also became an act of mentally and spiritually reaching out to acknowledge the Lord. He was acknowledging that the Lord is the supreme being, He is the God Almighty. My pastor's spirit was connecting with the Holy Spirit.

As we build intentional intimacy with God, we need to imagine ourselves aligning our spirit with heaven and acknowledging Jesus, Holy Spirit, or Father God. We can do this even in our busy lifestyles and workdays packed with meetings. All we need is that reminder to shift our mindset from business as usual to acknowledging that God is supreme over our day. And it only takes a moment to redirect your mind and let your spirit follow that shift.

It can be a learned skill, this intimacy. This is just a practical way of learning to be intentional. And just by saying His name, you shift the atmosphere of intentionality. You are saying to the Lord, I want this intimacy with You—even in this busy day.

Romans 12:2 says, "Do not conform to the pattern of this world, but be transformed by the renewing of your mind." To transform and renew also means to shift your mindset. By learning to shift your mind toward intimacy with God, you are leaning a new tool for transformation. And when your mind is transformed, everything else becomes naturally aligned to heaven.

In Colossians 3:1-4, we read, "Since, then, you have been raised with Christ, set your hearts on things above, where Christ is, seated at the right hand of God. Set your minds on things above, not on earthly things. For you died, and your life is now hidden with Christ in God. When Christ, who is your life, appears, then you also will appear with Him in glory." Give me an "amen" on that! Developing intentionality in intimacy with God is easy when you set your mind on things that are above your present situation. In fact, way above, like heavenward. God understands that we are busy during the day and that we have schedules to keep, bosses to keep happy, deadlines to meet. But it is the intentional mind shift that will create the intimacy that you desire. As you make the effort to lean into Him for intimacy, He will respond. I promise.

THERE IS ALWAYS MORE

With this guide to the feeler gift, you are experiencing the surface of the gift. You may be realizing there is a depth to this gift, and that you may be just scratching the surface of its potential and anointing. You may also realize that there is so much more to your relationship with God and that by pursuing intimacy with Him you are also growing in your understanding of the gifts he has given you!

Throughout this journey, you have learned basic tips to pray, intercede, to shield yourself, and to actually feel the atmosphere and be able to change it. You have also learned how to connect more intimately with God in order to continue developing your gift. Now it is time to practice these tips and pay attention to what the Lord is trying to teach you! Ask the Holy Spirit questions and rely upon His revelations.

As you grow and practice, please know that you are protected from the enemy, as long as you do not partner with that weasel. If you are relying upon God and trusting in the Lord Jesus for guidance and permission, then go forth. Do not fear. There is so much more to learn and understand!

We have covered a lot of Scripture so far, but I want to leave you with John 14. I call John chapter 14 the "in" chapter. The word "in" is written sixteen times. I encourage you to read this chapter to be in the "in" crowd. I would want to write down the whole chapter but here are some highlights:

John 14:1, "Do not let your hearts be troubled. You believe in God; believe also in me." Jesus goes on to say in verse 12-14, "Very truly I tell you, whoever believes in me will do the works I have been doing, and they will do even greater things than these, because I am going to the Father. And I will do whatever you ask in my name, so that the Father may be glorified in the Son. You may ask me for anything in my name, and I will do it."

John 14:15-17 says, "If you love Me, keep my commands. And I will ask the Father, and he will give you another advocate to help you and be with you forever—the Spirit of truth. The world cannot accept him, because it neither sees him nor knows him. But you know him, for he lives with you and will be in you."

Then, in John 14:23 we read, "Anyone who loves me will obey my teaching." And finally, verses 26-27, "But the Advocate, the Holy Spirit, whom the Father will send in my name, will teach you all things and will remind you of everything I have said to you. Peace I leave with you; my peace I give you. I do not give to you as the world gives. Do not let your hearts be troubled and do not be afraid." These are incredibly powerful words from Christ! Soak in them as you step further into your gift.

Before I leave you to carry on practicing and walking in your feeler gift, I want to share my commissioning word to you:

Go forth mighty warrior. Trust in the Lord and what He directs you to do. Pray mightily and declare in the atmosphere all the glorious things that the Lord is doing. Continue to ask the Lord for protection. He is trustworthy. I commission you in the mighty Name of Jesus Christ. You are His instrument. You are to partner with Him and co-labor your energy for this mission, your feelings, your emotions, and your healing; knowing that He is protecting you and instructing you to do His good works. He is trustworthy and He trusts you. Continue on this mission of learning and revelation through the Holy Scriptures and have a healthy friendship with Jesus Christ.

My prayer for you:

> *I speak the priestly blessing over you from Numbers 6:24-26. "The Lord bless you and keep you; the Lord make his face shine on you and be gracious to you; the Lord turn His face toward you and give you peace."*

> *Lord, I pray that every person who reads this book will be able to use the tools that they have learned. Lord, protect your sons and daughters. Give them new strategies to defeat the enemy and allow them to see themselves as you see them. You love us greatly and you are so kind to us. Thank you for your gifts and treasures that you give us. You are so generous. I give you my yes, and I surrender to you, my Lord. May everyone that reads this book be able to do the same. Amen.*

ACTIVATIONS

DEVELOPING DISCERNMENT
AND RECOGNIZING PATTERNS:

As an exercise, write down how you are feeling in the morning when you get up. It is easy to write one or two words. Then, begin to notice any changes throughout the day. Put a time and place next to your words. If you can tolerate the constant note taking, do this for seven days. Make a note whether the weekend was a routine weekend, or you experienced a special activity on your days off. When you have a moment, after the seven days, sit down and ask God to reveal any patterns to you. A pattern is similar feelings or emotions that surface in a certain time-period or a place.

FEELING ATMOSPHERES:

One way to experiment with this aspect of the feeler gift is to practice. When you get out of bed in the morning, take a moment to assess how you are feeling. You may feel drowsy, for example, but I encourage you to press into the *emotions* you are feeling. As you leave your house, is there any change? As you are in the car (with your radio off), assess again your feelings or mood.

Now, as you walk into the store, or the building you work in, stop and take a moment to assess the change in your feelings.

The next exercise is to pay attention when someone enters your space. When you are working alongside other people, lean into the change in the atmosphere. Is there a change? If so, how do your feelings change? Do your feelings change due to the fact you like or dislike that person? Write down the feelings you have around different individuals at that particular time frame. If you like or dislike that person, why? Use only one to two words to describe your emotions. Does the time of day make a difference when you feel that person? Use your feeler gift to intentionally feel the emotions or the soul of that person. The soul is where you carry your emotions.

CHECK YOURSELF AT THE DOOR:

When you check yourself at the door, you engage with the Holy Spirit and ask Him questions. This is the learning stage where He will begin to teach you. There are several questions that you need to ask:

1. What am I feeling? Pay attention to your different feelings and emotions.
2. Are these emotions mine? Is Holy Spirit trying to tell me something?
3. Are these feelings from someone else?
4. Are these feelings from the atmosphere around me?
5. Do I do anything about it (if it is coming from a person)? Or do I just pray? (Note: Always pray but know that there are times the Lord is directing you to do something specifically or intercede on a deeper level.)

CHANGING ATMOSPHERES:

Picture a radio in your mind. Feel what channel you are on. Now, reach up (in your mind) and begin to turn the channel. Turn the channel until you are connected to God, feeling the atmosphere you are standing in. What are you feeling?

Now, go through the list of questions to ask the Holy Spirit:

1. Is the feeling mine? (Make sure that the enemy is not trying to have you partner with the current atmosphere, like he may have done in the past.)
2. Is it from someone else? (You could be near a person and are feeling them.)
3. Is this feeling in the atmosphere?

Once you've assessed the atmosphere, pray the opposite emotion you are feeling and pray into the atmosphere one of the attributes of God. You are reversing and taking authority over the atmosphere.

I have used a simple wording for these moments: I take off and put back on. I take off what the enemy is doing, and I put back on the Lord's blessing (or opposite emotion). Whatever you take off, you must put something back on as a replacement, something that is of the Lord, such as peace, comfort, or love. We do not want the enemy to have the opportunity to put back his own stuff!

FEELING THE EMOTIONS OF OTHERS:

As you learn about the feeler gift and begin to feel others' emotions, practice on people you know. This gives you access to ask questions. For example, ask your co-workers, friends, or family if they are experiencing the emotion that you are sensing from them. Be open to their honest feedback—that is the best way to grow and learn!

As beginning feelers, we are often able to pick up on strong emotions easier, and unfortunately, they are usually negative emotions. Be sure to ask questions about other people's emotions with sensitivity and without intruding. But also, be ready for the explanations that may ensue. Being sensitive to what they are feeling sometimes means you just need to listen. Just because you feel an emotion correctly does not mean it is the time to solve their problems.

EXCHANGING LIES FOR TRUTH:

Take a piece of paper and fold it lengthwise so that it creates two columns. You can also do this in your journal. At the top of the left column, write the word "Lies." Remember the prayer to hear God's voice? Find it in this book and say that prayer. Then ask the Lord: "Lord, please bring to my mind the lies I am believing." Write a word or two that comes to mind and skip a line between each lie that is revealed. Write until the Lord stops speaking. Really press in to listen for these lies to be revealed.

Now, place your hand over that part of the paper that contains these lies and say a prayer of repentance. In your own words, the prayer should include the following:

1. Thank God for His answers that He gave you.
2. Repent for believing the lies that Satan and his minions have told you.
3. Repent for taking on the emotions that are associated with those lies.
4. Repent and ask forgiveness for partnering your responses or reactions to these lies.

For the second part to this exercise, write the word "Truth" at the top of the other column. For each lie that the Lord exposed, I want you to ask the Lord for HIS truth. Write His truth to every single lie that was put on the paper. Thank the Lord for His revelation. Take a pair of scissors and cut the paper in half, cutting off the lie section. Rip it into shreds. They no longer exist. You are no longer walking in the reality of the lies. Every day, for the next thirty days, I want you to declare the truths over yourself. You are beginning to change your mindset of what you used to walk in. Daily declare your identity into the atmosphere. Say them out loud. Hang them on your mirror, if needed, and declare them in the heavens every day. Your new identity of truth is being formed into your mind and soul. You are transforming your mind. You have reason to celebrate!

BATTLING THE DEMONIC

Remember to always say prayers out loud when directing it towards the enemy. You can practice this by praying out loud to the Lord in your own devotional time. The more accustomed you are to praying out loud, the easier it becomes.

BUILDING A RELATIONSHIP
AND INTIMACY WITH GOD

Be intentional with your engagement with the Lord. Not only spending time with Him during your devotions but choosing to be intentional to turn your mind to Him throughout the day. Set timers on your phone to remind yourself to turn your thoughts to Him. Even during a busy workday, as you reach out to turn off the phone alarm, reach out with your mind and acknowledge God. Simply say one of His attributes, or His Name, and that is your engagement with Him.

Here are some other ways develop your intimacy with God:

- Be in the Bible every day. Afterall, it is our daily bread!
- Spend time just being in God's presence.
- Ask Him questions.
- Become His friend.

Made in the USA
Monee, IL
18 February 2022

91435291R00085